AFRICAN ETHNOGRAPHIC STUDIES OF THE 20TH CENTURY

Volume 41

KIKUYU

KIKUYU
Social and Political Institutions

H. E. LAMBERT

LONDON AND NEW YORK

First published in 1956 by Oxford University Press for the International African Institute.

This edition first published in 2018
by Routledge
2 Park Square, Milton Park, Abingdon, Oxon OX14 4RN

and by Routledge
711 Third Avenue, New York, NY 10017

Routledge is an imprint of the Taylor & Francis Group, an informa business

© 1956 International African Institute

All rights reserved. No part of this book may be reprinted or reproduced or utilised in any form or by any electronic, mechanical, or other means, now known or hereafter invented, including photocopying and recording, or in any information storage or retrieval system, without permission in writing from the publishers.

Trademark notice: Product or corporate names may be trademarks or registered trademarks, and are used only for identification and explanation without intent to infringe.

British Library Cataloguing in Publication Data
A catalogue record for this book is available from the British Library

ISBN: 978-0-8153-8713-8 (Set)
ISBN: 978-0-429-48813-9 (Set) (ebk)
ISBN: 978-1-138-59553-8 (Volume 41) (hbk)
ISBN: 978-0-429-48821-4 (Volume 41) (ebk)

Publisher's Note
The publisher has gone to great lengths to ensure the quality of this reprint but points out that some imperfections in the original copies may be apparent.

Disclaimer
The publisher has made every effort to trace copyright holders and would welcome correspondence from those they have been unable to trace.

KIKUYU
SOCIAL AND POLITICAL
INSTITUTIONS

BY

H. E. LAMBERT

Published for the
INTERNATIONAL AFRICAN INSTITUTE
by the
OXFORD UNIVERSITY PRESS
LONDON   NEW YORK   TORONTO
1956

Oxford University Press, Amen House, London E.C.4

GLASGOW   NEW YORK   TORONTO   MELBOURNE   WELLINGTON
BOMBAY   CALCUTTA   MADRAS   KARACHI   CAPE TOWN   IBADAN

Geoffrey Cumberlege, Publisher to the University

Printed in Great Britain by
The Camelot Press Ltd., London and Southampton

FOREWORD

THIS portion of a much longer unpublished work on the social and political institutions of the tribes of the Kikuyu Land Unit, is being issued now in view of the current interest in Kikuyu affairs. I am much indebted to Dr. L. S. B. Leakey for allowing me to read his remarkable study of the Southern Kikuyu, unfortunately not yet published; to Mr. W. H. Laughton for the loan of his pioneer work, *An Introductory Study of the Meru People*, also unpublished; and to the late Reverend Philip M'Inoto for a copy of his unpublished *Asili ya Wameru na Tabia Zao*. My gratitude is due to very many Africans for their willing and patient help; and in particular to Messrs. M'Muras Kairangi of Meru, Kofia Migwi of Fort Hall, and Munyambo Kirata of Kiambu. Finally, I wish to express my thanks to Professor I. Schapera for his sustained encouragement, and to Mrs. E. M. Chilver and Dr. L. P. Mair for their generous help in the preparation of the manuscript.

Most of the material for this study was collected during my residence in Kenya as an Administrative Officer.

H.E.L.

CONTENTS

	FOREWORD	v
1.	THE TRIBES OF THE UNIT	1
2.	GENERAL TERMS DENOTING AGE	3
3.	THE REGIMENTAL SYSTEM (KIKUYU, EMBU, MERU)	8
4.	PRE-INITIATION AGE-SETS	32
5.	THE GENERATION	40
6.	RITUALS OF THE AGE ORGANIZATION	53
7.	SOCIAL FUNCTIONS OF THE AGE ORGANIZATION	66
8.	MILITARY FUNCTIONS OF THE AGE ORGANIZATION	69
9.	POLITICAL FUNCTIONS OF THE AGE ORGANIZATION	73

Pre-Initiation Institutions; Warriors' Institutions; Elders' Institutions; Fees in Kikuyu; The Higher Grades in Meru; Correspondence between the different systems; Women's Institutions; Leadership; The Judicial System; The *ad hoc* Bench in Kikuyu; Principles of Justice; Judicial Oaths; Enforcement of Judgements; Essentials of the Judicial System; Legislation.

SKETCH MAP OF THE KIKUYU LAND UNIT	145
INDEX	147

I

THE TRIBES OF THE UNIT

THE area of the Kikuyu Land Unit is defined by the Native Lands Trust Ordinance of 1938, and comprises the five administrative districts of Fort Hall, Nyeri, Kiambu, Meru and Embu. Its total African population in 1948 was 1,259,830. They fall into the four main tribal groups, speaking closely related languages, of Kikuyu, Meru, Chuka, and Embu. Each of these is further sub-divided into named territorial sections, the inhabitants of which are politically autonomous; these will be referred to as sub-tribes. The KIKUYU proper fall into three sub-tribes, *Metume* in Fort Hall, *Karura* in Kiambu and *Gaki* in Nyeri; closely related sub-tribes are the *Gichugu* and *Ndia* of Embu District. The EMBU themselves are divided into *Embu* and *Mbere*. The Meru and Chuka are both included in Meru District. The MERU proper are divided into *Imenti*, *Tigania* and *Igembe*. The *Igoji* and *Mwimbi* sub-tribes are closely related to the Meru. Of the other sub-tribes of this district the *Miutini* and *Muthambi* have affinities with both Meru and Chuka, as do the *Tharaka*, some of whom live in the Kamba Land Unit.

These peoples have in common certain general principles of social structure. Descent is patrilineal and marriage in general patrilocal. Political organization rests on the grouping of the male population according to age. Age-sets are formed at the time of their initiation into manhood; successive sets are combined into larger units to which I give the name of regiment, and these

2   KIKUYU SOCIAL AND POLITICAL INSTITUTIONS

again are grouped in generations. In Meru the women too are grouped in age-sets. This grouping is anticipated by the naming of groups of age-mates while they are still too young for initiation. Individuals, male or female, can be described at every period of life by terms denoting age and the attainment of the status held to be appropriate to any given age.

Territorial organization is based on the joint rights of an extended family (Kikuyu *mbari*) in an area of land (Kikuyu *githaka*) over which its homesteads are scattered; they are not grouped in compact villages. A *githaka* area with its inhabitants, including both right-holders and attached dependants, is called in Kikuyu *itura*, and is the smallest political unit. I translate this word 'village group'. A group of these was known in Kikuyu as *mwaki*, which may be translated 'neighbourhood', and for certain purposes, including the formation of age-regiments, a number of these combined in a wider unit for which there is no Kikuyu term.[1]

[1] For particulars of the populations of the tribal groups and their distribution see Middleton, J., *The Kikuyu and Kamba of Kenya* (Ethnographic Survey of Africa, East Central Africa, Part V) International African Institute, 1953.

2

GENERAL TERMS DENOTING AGE

In all tribes of the Unit the social status of an individual, as determined by age, sex, the right to procreate, and parenthood, is denoted by a generic term applied to him and to all others of a like standing in society. Certain of the terms used do not distinguish sex for very young or very old people, that is, well before sex has begun to be biologically functional in character and well after it can be reasonably supposed to have ceased to be so.

The following are the terms most commonly used. An infant, a recently born baby, is called *gakenge* (pl. *tukenge*) in Kikuyu, and *gakenke* (pl. *tukenke*) in the Meru group and Chuka. The word *rukenge, rukenke,* is similarly used. Both terms are normally applied to a child up to the time it begins to toddle, and may be used of it as long as it is breast-fed.

In the next stage, from the time it starts to walk up to the time it is considered old enough to help in herding goats or in its mother's household chores, it is called *kaana* (pl. *twana*) throughout the unit. The word *mwana* (Kikuyu pl. *chiana*, Meru pl. *sana*), from the same stem, is used much more generally of any child and, like the English 'child', can mean the offspring of whatever age of the person mentioned; for example, in Meru *mwana wa mukenye wetu*, 'child of our girl', may refer to the child, possibly grown up, of the speaker's daughter or sister, with the meaning 'our relative on the female side'.

A small boy is called *kahi* (pl. *tuhi*) or *kahii* (pl. *tuhii*) in

4 KIKUYU SOCIAL AND POLITICAL INSTITUTIONS

Kikuyu.[1] Such a youngster is considered old enough to be subject to functional differentiation in regard to sex; for instance, he will start herding goats. But the functional differentiation is still slight, and it is not unusual to see small girls herding goats. A small girl is *karigu* (pl. *turigu*) in Kikuyu, *gakenye* (pl. *tukenye*) in Meru, and *kathera* (pl. *tuthera*) in Chuka.

An older boy who is not yet circumcised is *kihi* or *kihii* (pl. *ihi, ihii*) in Kikuyu, *mwiji* (pl. *biiji*) in Meru, and *kivisi* (pl. *ivisi*) in Chuka, and an older girl who is not yet initiated is *kirigu* (pl. *irigu*) in Kikuyu, *mukenye* (pl. *nkenye*) in Meru and *muthera* (pl. *mithera*) in Chuka. Nowadays *kirigu* is used in Kikuyu as a term of contempt for an uncircumcised married woman; it expresses, of course, her real status in the tribal system, in which there is a greater differentiation between the circumcised and the uncircumcised than between the married and the unmarried.

There is normally a considerable difference of actual age between the Meru *mukenye* and the Chuka *muthera* on the one hand and the Kikuyu *kirigu* and Tharaka *mukenye* on the other, because among Meru and Chuka initiation is normally a pre-nuptial rite, while with Kikuyu and Tharaka it takes place before menstruation. In all these tribes marriage is unusual before the girl is fully grown.

The word *mukenye*, used with reference to a woman's natal group, can express her relationship to that group long after she has passed the actual status of *mukenye*. In this respect its use is similar to that of the English 'daughter'. A woman remains a *mukenye* of her own clan for ever, whereas she is a *muchieri* or *mweikuru* of the clan into which she has married. Thus a man may say, "So-and-So is a great-great-grandchild of our *mukenye*." *Mwana wa*

---

[1] *Kahii* appears to be the original form of the word. *Kaiji* (pl. *twiji*) in Meru, and *kavisi* (pl. *twisi*) in Chuka.

GENERAL TERMS DENOTING AGE 5

mukenye wetu means normally the legitimate child of a woman who belonged, before she was married, to our family, but *mwana wa mukenye* means the son or daughter of an uninitiated girl, in fact an illegitimate child.

The Meru call a well-developed boy, considered old enough to join in battle though still uncircumcised, *mwiji wa ndinguri*, and a big 'bouncing' girl, still uninitiated, *ndinguri ya mukenye*. Girls who have not yet undergone the rite of clitoridectomy, but have had their ears pierced and their bodies scarred, are called *nthamari*. They are still *nkenye* and remain *nkenye* until the final initiatory rite.

In the Meru groups a recently circumcised youth is called *ntani* (pl. *ntani*) and a recently circumcised girl, during her period of seclusion and up to the time of her marriage, is called *ngutu* (pl. *ngutu*). A recently widowed woman is also called *ngutu*; the word signifies a female who is initiated, but not living with a man.

In Chuka a young man or girl who has been recently initiated is called *kichere* (pl. *ichere*) while the operation wound remains unhealed. The Kikuyu term for a boy or girl who has just been initiated is *kiumiri* (pl. *chiumiri*).

The Kikuyu call an initiated but still unmarried young man *mwanake* (pl. *aanake*). This word is also used for 'warrior'. A bachelor is *mundu wa mumo*, and an unmarried girl *muiritu wa mumo*, and *mumo* is used of both sexes collectively. In strict usage a *mundu wa mumo* becomes a *mwanake* when he has made certain payments to the preceding grade of warriors, and a *muiritu* ceases to be *wa mumo* when young men initiated at the same time as herself become *aanake*. A small initiated girl is called *kairitu* (pl. *tuiritu*) and an older one, who is not yet married, *muiritu* (pl. *airitu*).

In the Meru group an initiated young man, still

6 KIKUYU SOCIAL AND POLITICAL INSTITUTIONS

unmarried or married recently, is called *muthaka* (pl. *nthaka*). He belongs to the warrior grade. In Chuka the word is *nthaka* in both singular and plural.

In Tharaka, where girls are initiated before menstruation, an initiated unmarried girl is called *itiga* (pl. *matiga*). In Chuka, an initiated girl is *mwari* (pl. *chiari*) until she becomes a *muka mukuru* (pl. *aka akuru*), a mature woman, that is, has children.

A bride is called *muhiki* (pl. *ahiki*) in Kikuyu, and the same word (in the form *muiki*, pl. *aiki*) is used in Meru and Tharaka. In Meru a young married woman who has borne a child is called *muchieri* (pl. *achieri*) until, at the next handing-over ceremony (*ntuiko* or *rukunyi*), her husband's *nthuki* goes up one grade in age status. She is then called *mweikuru* (pl. *aikuru*). This term is, however, more strictly confined to a wife of an elder of the ruling set.[1]

A young married man of the set below the ruling set is called in Meru *muruao* (pl. *miruao*). The *miruao* in 1946 were of the *Kiruja* (*Michubu*) set. The word appears to be derived from the Masai *ol-muruo*.

In the Meru group *mukuru* (pl. *akuru*) is used of a man who has children or whose contemporaries have children. A *mukuru* in strict usage is a man whose first child is old enough to be circumcised, but the word is often used playfully of a youngster or respectfully of any middle-aged man. In Kikuyu *muthuri* (pl. *athuri*) is similarly used. In Tharaka a woman with a child old enough to be circumcised is *mweikuru* (pl. *eikuru*). In Kikuyu a married woman with children is called *mutumia*[2] (pl. *atumia*) or

---

[1] See below.

[2] The same word, *mutumia*, is used in Kamba to denote a male elder. In strict usage in Kikuyu a *mutumia* is a woman with a circumcised child. The intermediate stage between *muhiki* and *mutumia* is *mundu muka* which term, meaning simply 'female person', includes, however, a *muhiki* or a *mutumia*.

GENERAL TERMS DENOTING AGE 7

mutimia (pl. *atimia*). A woman with no circumcised child is known as *mutumia wa kang'ei*. Generally speaking in Kikuyu a bride remains a *muhiki* until she has a child, and then becomes a *mutumia*; a woman whose first child has been fully initiated (circumcised) is known as *mutumia wa nyakinyua* (pl. *atumia a nyakinyua*).[1]

In the Meru group a grandmother—that is a woman who has completed her life-cycle—is called *ntichio* (pl. *ntichio*). The original meaning of the word appears to be 'mother of a mother', but it is often used of any aged woman. Throughout the Meru group and Chuka a very aged man or woman is called *ntindiri* (pl. *ntindiri*), a word derived from *tindira*, 'endure, persist, grow old'.

In Kikuyu *kiheti*[2] (pl. *iheti*) means a woman past child-bearing; in Gichugu and Ndia *mwongia* (pl. *ongia*) is also used with the same meaning. In all Kikuyu a very aged woman is called *kiguguta* (pl. *iguguta*); this word can also be used of very aged men or very aged cattle. An old man is *muthuri mukuru* (pl. *athuri akuru*) and an old woman *mutumia mukuru* (pl. *atumia akuru*). In Gichugu, Ndia, and Gaki very aged persons are sometimes called *mitindiri*; I have not heard this word anywhere else in Kikuyu.

---

[1] This term refers to the right of a woman who has reached this status to drink intoxicating liquor. In some areas she only acquires this status when she has two initiated children.

[2] This word (in the form *kiveti*) is used in Kamba to denote an established wife, that is, one who has a child and has been allotted her own place to cultivate.

3

THE REGIMENTAL SYSTEM

Kikuyu

IN Kikuyu sets of boys initiated at one time used to be grouped in larger sets, each with a specific name, which may conveniently be called regiments. The Kikuyu proper (Gaki, Metume and Karura) applied the same word, *riika* (pl. *mariika*), to a regiment as to an initiation-set, but the Gichugu and Ndia called the set *irua* (pl. *marua*) and the regiment *riika* (pl. *mariika*). A somewhat similar grouping was customary in Embu and Mbere, where the word for a set is *karua* (pl. *turua*), and for a regiment *irua* (pl. *marua*).

There were at least five distinct methods of grouping in different parts of Kikuyu. In all of them the magic pertaining to numbers was taken into consideration. In most of northern Kikuyu the period for the formation of a regiment was thirteen years. But the magic of the 'blessed' number, nine, was imported into the method of formation. In Gichugu, Ndia, and Tetu this was done by leaving the last nine years of the period entirely free from male initiations, all the warriors of the regiment having been circumcised during the first four years. The closed period was known as *muhingo*. The name of the first set was fairly regularly taken as the regimental name.

The system can be illustrated for Gichugu and Ndia as follows:

THE REGIMENTAL SYSTEM

Years	Sets	Regiment
1889	Ngungi	
1890	Mutuakamuru	
1891	Nguo ya Nyina	NGUNGI
1892	Kienjeku	
1893-1901	(only girls' sets)	
1902	Wakanene	(Start of Wakanene regiment)

Occasionally a set was distinguished from a regiment of the same name by the addition of a qualifying phrase. Thus the set Ngungi was known as Ngungi ya Miti-iguru ('The Ngungi of the Up-Trees') in reference to the Masai raids of the times, during which the Ndia warriors hid themselves up trees and met the raiders with showers of arrows.

The following regimental names are still remembered by the elders in Gichugu and Ndia. The dates have been calculated on the basis of the statements that Europeans first entered their country between Ngungi and Wakanene and that the latter regiment started to be formed just after the great famine (Ng'aragu ya Ruraya, about 1900).

Years	Regiments	Years	Regiments
1902-5	Wakanene	1824-7	Kang'ethe
1889-92	Ngungi	1811-14	Njorobe
1876-9	Watuke	1798-1801	Mugacho
1863-6	Kiambuthi	1785-8	Nduriri
1850-3	Manyaki	1772-5	Kinuthia
1837-40	Gitau	1759-62	Karanja

A few names of still earlier regiments are remembered by some elders, but as none of my informants was certain of their order in seniority, I have omitted them.

It is occasionally suggested that at one time or in one area the Ndia followed another system, also based on the regimental period of thirteen years. In this system, if it existed at all, one *irua* of males was circumcised every

B

10 KIKUYU SOCIAL AND POLITICAL INSTITUTIONS

year for five years; then came a gap of two years during which no males were circumcised, a further period of five years each with its own *irua*, and a gap of one year before the next regiment was started. The earlier division was known as *nene* ('large') and the other as *nini* ('small'). Only one informant described this arrangement to me in any detail and the other elders present disagreed with him. There is, however, a note in the Political Record (dated December 1913) which reads:

In each Rika there are two divisions designated as nini and nenne with generally an interval of about two years. Waka-nenne is an exception to this, there being only one age of this Rika, the youths of Nzanga time gave themselves this name but the elders regard them as Wakanenne nini.

The system in the Tetu area of Nyeri district was identical with that which was normal in Ndia, viz. the circumcision of males once a year for four years followed by a gap (*muhingo*, prohibition) of a further nine years before a new regiment was started.

The following names of regiments are remembered in Tetu. Some elders give a few more, but as they themselves admit, these must be regarded as somewhat doubtful.

The list given here may be taken as substantially correct:

Years	Regiments	Years	Regiments
1925-8	Muthetha	1837-40	Ndirangu
1915-18	Mbauni	1824-7	Ndigirige
1902-5	Ndumia	1811-14	Ndiang'ue
1889-92	Ndung'u	1798-1801	Theuri
1876-9	Ndiiritu	1785-8	Matu
1863-6	Mangucha	1772-5	Tatua
1850-3	King'ore	1759-62	Thuita

THE REGIMENTAL SYSTEM

The regiments are described as right-hand (*tatane*) and left-hand (*gitienye*) alternately. Ndiiritu, Ndumia and Muthetha, for example, are *tatane* and Mangucha, Ndung'u and Mbauni *gitienye*. The elders liken this arrangement to the division of a man's sons alternately between his own and their mother's families so far as the 'inherited' names are concerned. But they say that it is an imitation of the Masai system, and the terms are certainly those the Masai use of their right and left-hand circumcision groups (*etatene* and *ekedyanye*). No functional importance appears to be attached to the division.

The first set of every regiment was called *murichu* and the other three were grouped together as *muchenge*.

The system is illustrated by the following plan of the last few regiments in Tetu.

Years	GITIENYE			TATANE		
	Sets		Regiments	Sets		Regiments
	Murichu	Muchenge		Murichu	Muchenge	
1863	Mangucha					
1864		Watuka				
1865		Ngithua	MANGUCHA			
1866		Kaguru-Keru				
1867-75	(Period of Muhingo. Only girls initiated)					
1876				Ndiiritu		
1877					Ngororo	NDIIRITU
1878					Heho	
1879					Ndoboka	
1880-8	(Period of Muhingo. Only girls initiated)					
1889	Ndung'u					
1890		Nyuguto	NDUNG'U			
1891		Kimani				
1892		Haba				
1893-1901	(Period of Muhingo. Only girls initiated)					

12 KIKUYU SOCIAL AND POLITICAL INSTITUTIONS

1902		Itumia ⎫
1903		Nyasa
		(Kianyungu) ⎬ NDUMIA
1904		Njuu
1905		Kamunya ⎭
1906-14	(Period of Muhingo.	Only girls initiated)
1915	Mbauni ⎫	
1916	Mikenga	
1917	Nyambari ⎬ MBAUNI	
1918	Kianduma ⎭	
1919-24	(Period of Muhingo.	Only girls initiated)
1925		Muthetha ⎫
1926		Muthaithi
1927		Kiareri ⎬ MUTHETHA
1928		Kamano ⎭

The shortening of the gap between the Mbauni and Muthetha regiments to six years is indicative, the elders say, of the change in attitude brought about by European influences. In the original system many initiates in the *murichu* set of any regiment would be full-grown men. But after the 1914-18 war youths were expected to pay tax from the apparent age of sixteen years. To the African this was a political matter, and no uncircumcised person could play a part in politics. The youths themselves were reluctant to perform the duties of adult men while they were debarred by tribal custom from the corresponding privileges. But the local officers of Government, having no knowledge of the customary period of prohibition, concluded that the youths were deliberately delaying circumcision in order to avoid payment of the tax. Eventually the elders rescinded the prohibition, and thereafter boys were initiated almost every year as girls are. Muthetha was the last regiment to be formed.

There is some doubt about the name of the *murichu* set of the Ndung'u regiment. One elder, himself of Ndung'u,

THE REGIMENTAL SYSTEM

called it simply *murichu*. The other elders present said it must have been Ndung'u. But the word means 'smallpox' or 'pock-marked people' and the date given by Routledge,[1] following McGregor, for the set (Mutung'u) in Fort Hall and Kiambu named after the smallpox epidemic is 1894. It is possible that the epidemic started earlier in Nyeri or that the regiment still in power at the time changed its name or had it changed by others to fit this most important of events. But comparison with other lists suggests that there was a difference of no more than a year or two between the northern set Ndung'u and the southern set Mutung'u and that the order given for the former is correct. The process of regiment formation of Tetu is much more regular than that followed farther south, and some of the later dates in Tetu are known with considerable probability. I shall therefore take the northern Ndung'u date as very nearly right for the southern set Mutung'u, but on the understanding that for sets before, say, 1900, this may involve an error, either in the north or in the south (probably, if at all, the latter) of anything up to five years in the dates recorded. That Routledge's date (1894) for Mtung'u is several years too late is suggested by the statement of Karura elders of that set that most of them had married and some of them had children four or five years old before the Ruraya famine started.

At least three other systems obtained elsewhere in Nyeri district. In Agothi the period was thirteen years and the final regimental names were the same as those in Tetu. But there was no *muhingo*, and the circumcision of the first set of a new regiment could take place in the year following that of the last male set of the previous one. Magical considerations were reflected in the number of sets, that is, the number of male circumcision years during

[1] *With a Prehistoric People*, 1910, p. 11.

14 KIKUYU SOCIAL AND POLITICAL INSTITUTIONS

the period of formation. There were never more than nine sets in a regiment. The regimental periods coincided with those of Tetu and the names of the sets initiated in the first four years corresponded with those of Tetu. If in any one of these years only girls were initiated, the girls' set received the Tetu name, while the boys' set formed in the next year received the name of the fourth Tetu set. Thus the Ndung'u regiment in Ndothi includes no Kimani set, as this name was given to girls only. The nine male sets were spread over the thirteen-year period, the four years in which no boys were circumcised being spaced fairly evenly between them.

Years	Sets	Regiment
1889	Ndung'u	
1890	Nyuguto	
1892	Haba	
1893	Ndutu	
1896	Mukururo	NDUNG'U
1897	Kaibang'a	
1899	Kiinami	
1900	Murariri	
1901	Rubia	
1902	Ndumia	Start of Ndumia Regiment

Informants' accounts of this system are not unanimous. There is general agreement that each regiment consisted of nine sets, but some deny that the regular period for the formation of a regiment was thirteen years. It appears, however, that a regiment regularly consists of nine male sets.

The original system of regiment formation in Mathira differed widely from that of all the rest of Kikuyu, except possibly parts of Gichugu and Ndia. The basic period of thirteen years still held, but with less precision than in Tetu. In Mathira it was doubled, that is one regimental period covered approximately two regimental periods in

THE REGIMENTAL SYSTEM 15

Tetu. Five sets were initiated during a period of twenty-one years (thus founding the regiment on the sacred number seven). These were spaced more or less evenly through the period so that there was usually a gap of about four years (nine seasons) between successive sets. At the end of the twenty-one year period there was another gap of four years (nine seasons) during which no initiation of boys took place. It would seem that there was no actual prohibition against circumcision in the interval between two sets in the twenty-one year period. Any set formed in this interval would be absorbed in the previous set, though it might be known temporarily by the name of a permanent set circumcised outside Mathira during the same year. The total period, including the four-year gap after the completion of the regiment, was twenty-five years, approximately double that in Tetu. The final name of a regiment was usually that of its first set, but the alternating names were commonly employed. These were Ngunjiri and Ndirangu.

Years	Sets	Regiment
1885	Ngigi	End of Ngunjiri Regiment
1886-9	(only girls' sets)	
1890	Nyuguto	
1893	Nuthi	
1899	Kiinami	NDIRANGU
1905	Wakaba	
1910	Njaramba	
1911-14	(only girls' sets)	
1915	Mbauni	Start of Ngunjiri Regiment

Two successive sets, if very close together, were sometimes given a common name. Thus Nyuguto and Nuthi are both referred to as Nyuguto, and Ngigi and the previous set, Karonda, are sometimes known as Thugu.

Lists collected in Gikondi, in the south of Nyeri district,

16 KIKUYU SOCIAL AND POLITICAL INSTITUTIONS

indicate a regimental period of twenty-one years which is not followed by a gap before the opening of a new regiment. Each regiment contained seven sets. The first three were grouped together as Murichu and the other four as Muchenge. The name of a regiment was normally that of the first set. The terms *tatane* and *gitienye* were applied alternately to regiments and the alternating system of naming was in vogue.

Years		*Sets*		*Regiments*
? 1868	Murichu	Gichagwa		
1871		Wanyaga		
1874		Githuku		NDIRANGU or MANGUCHA
				(*gitienye*)
1877	Muchenge,	Ngororo		
? 1880		Njarura		
1884		Bari		
1888		Nyongo		
1889	Murichu,	Ndung'u		
1892		Haba		
1899		Kiinami		NGUNJIRI or NDIIRITU or
				NDUNG'U
1902	Muchenge,	Ndumia		(*tatane*)
1904		Mitaroni		
1905		Kanyuto		
1909		Thimu		
1910		Njaramba		(Start of Ndirangu or Mangucha or Njaramba regiment (*gitienye*)

In Othaya, another area of Nyeri district, the regiment consisted of seven sets. It appears that there was a gap of three years, that is, seven seasons, between the last set of a regiment and the first set of the next, but I am not certain of this. The period of formation was approximately thirteen years. I am told (though again I am not certain)

THE REGIMENTAL SYSTEM 17

that this same gap of seven seasons was the normal one in the southern portion of Muhito, also in Nyeri district. A list of sets in one regiment there was given me as follows:

Years	Sets	Regiment
1880	Ngaruiya	
1882	Chong'e	
1885	Ngigi	
1887	Kihengere	
1888	Nyongo	MBIRA
1889	Mutung'u	
1890	Nyuguto	
1891	Machoya	
1892	Haba	

It will be noticed that the period of formation was approximately thirteen years and that there were nine sets to a regiment. This method was very similar to that employed further south, including Karura. Indeed the name Mbira was the name of a Karura regiment. But the two Mbira regiments were 'out of step' by some three sets, or, in the estimated dates, three years.

The essentials of the southern system were a period of formation of approximately thirteen years, during which nine sets were initiated, followed by a gap of four years, that is, nine seasons. The emphasis was therefore on the 'blessed' number nine. Two consecutive sets were commonly linked together, particularly if they were initiated in consecutive years. This coupling was described by the word *kuruanithira*, 'to cause to be circumcised together'. The odd set, which had no mate, was known as *riika ria mwaga*, 'the set on its own, the odd set out'. Normally, it was the first set of the regiment because that was the largest, consisting as it did of all the young men who had

18 KIKUYU SOCIAL AND POLITICAL INSTITUTIONS

reached an initiable age during the previous nine seasons. The formal pattern was thus:

1st year	„	A
2nd	„	Girls only
3rd	„	B
4th	„	B1
5th	„	Girls only
6th	„	C
7th	„	C1
8th	„	Girls only
9th	„	D
10th	„	D1
11th	„	Girls only
12th	„	E
13th	„	E1

However, the period of formation could be lengthened considerably or shortened slightly and the 'odd set' might in practice be formed at any time. The formation of a set in the appropriate year might be impossible on account of famine or enemy attacks, or merely for lack of an adequate number of candidates. There were in fact considerable divergences from the ideal pattern in the formation of the last three regiments in Karura.

Years		*Sets*		*Regiments*
	1860	Guchu		
?	1862	Nguo ya Nyina		
?	1863	Muthuru		
	1865	Mwiruri		
?	1866	Wakirutu		MBUGWA
	1867	Kiambuthi		
	1869	Ngugi		
	1870	Kiriira		
	1872	Ruhang'a		
	1873-6	(Period of Muhingo. Only girls initiated)		

THE REGIMENTAL SYSTEM

1877	Wanyoike	
1878	Boro	
1879	Kiniti	
1880	Ngaruiya	NJENGA or MBIRA ITIMU
1881	Kianjagi	
1883	Mburu	
1884	Uhere	
1885	Ngigi	
1889	Mutung'u	
1890-3	(Period of Muhingo. Only girls initiated)	
1894	Kienjeku	
1897	Muthura	
1898-	(Famine. In-	
1900	dividual girls initiated as necessary)	
1901	Kamande	NJUNG'E
1903	Gatiti	
1904	Njege	
1905	Kanyutu	
1906	Nyarigi	
1907	Kang'ei	
1908	Matiba	
1909	Thigingi	Start of 'Githiga' Regiment

The Njung'e regiment was dislocated, not only by the great Famine (Ng'aragu ya Ruraya) but by the increasing intervention of the British, and there is some doubt as to when it could be deemed to have been completed. If all the sets named were male sets, as they are said to have been, the regiment should have ended with Matiba. But a considerable number of elders hold that it includes Thigingi. There was certainly no closed period after either Matiba or Thigingi. Perhaps for this reason certain elders include in Njung'e the following set, Makio, initiated in 1910; Ugimbi (1911) and Mwande (1912) were female sets. But the fact is that any attempt at regularity had by then been abandoned, and the following 'regiment',

20 KIKUYU SOCIAL AND POLITICAL INSTITUTIONS

known as Githiga, cannot accurately be called a regiment at all, although some elders say that it ends at Chiringi ('Shilling', 1923) and others at Ndege ('Aeroplane', 1926). There is no longer any fixed number of sets in a regiment nor any closed period between regiments. No 'regiment' subsequent to Githiga has been named, though there has been more than ample time. Those elders who fix an end for Githiga say that the following sets are *mumo*. The original method of regiment formation must now be admitted to have broken down completely.[1]

Sets containing girls only received distinguishing names unless the numbers of candidates were very small. The girls' sets between the Njenga and Njung'e regiments were:

1890	Githeri
1891	Kagicha (named after a dance)
1892	Kibiri or Kiangwachi ('sweet potato')
1893	Ndutu or Nuthi ('jigger flea')

The tentative dates given above differ considerably from those in previously published lists and from those given in the Political Records. On the whole the lists of sets given here cover a longer period. The most obvious reason for the difference is that the compilers of earlier lists took no account of the closed period between successive regiments. This is offset to some extent by the inclusion of regimental names in addition to set names, particularly in the south. Even the names of generations were included in several of the lists. Such interpolations were not, however, sufficient to make up for the omission of the closed periods.

---

[1] The elders of northern Metume do not recognize Githiga as a regimental name; they apply it to 'the younger married men'. In Gaki the word was used of the senior regiment by a newly completed one.

THE REGIMENTAL SYSTEM

The name given to a set usually recalls some circumstance which has caught the public fancy not long before, generally within a year of its initiation. When this can be dated the set too can be dated with fair accuracy. Thus Chiringi ('Shilling', 1923) recalls the introduction of the shilling into the Kenya currency, and Ndege (from Swahili, 'bird') the appearance of aeroplanes in Kenya in 1926. It is not, however, so easy to date earlier sets though the events their names commemorate may be known. Nuthi (Ndutu) may, for instance, recall the first appearance of the chigoe in Kikuyu, but we do not know exactly when that was; or it may recall a year when the fleas were particularly numerous, or when the candidates were specially afflicted by them. The names, moreover, may be purely local; a set name in Kiambu may be quite unknown in Nyeri. Where, however, the same name is used over a wide area, fairly accurate dating is possible.

I have taken the system as it was in Tetu as a basis for comparison because of its regularity. I have taken the Kiareri set as a starting-point. This was named Reri (Railway), because the Nairobi-Nanyuki railway reached the vicinity of Karatina not long before the set was circumcised. It was probably therefore initiated in 1926 or 1927. Another Tetu set, Kianduma ('Darkness'), was named after an eclipse which occurred, the younger elders say, in 1917. Accordingly I have dated the set at 1918. Using either of these sets as a fixed point and following the Tetu system and the order given by the elders, we must date the Tetu set Muthetha at 1925. This name is scarcely known at all in southern Kikuyu, where the 1925 set is usually called Mukwanju ('Walking Stick'). But in the list of sets as known in Limuru, given by Mr W. E. D. Knight in his evidence to the Land Commission (Evidence, Vol. I, p. 901), Muthetha appears as the set for 1925.

22 KIKUYU SOCIAL AND POLITICAL INSTITUTIONS

This affords some confirmation of the Tetu dating.

It is in the earlier dates in the Karura list particularly that I may have spaced the sets too widely. But it is worth remarking that the Tetu elders identify their Ndii-ritu regiment (started in 1876) with the Njenga regiment of Karura, which was started in 1877 according to my list. Mr Knight, in his evidence to the Land Commission, gives an actual instance of the length of time between the circumcision years of an elder and his son, belonging respectively to the Ngigi and Matiba sets. The date he gives for the latter is 1908, which can be taken as certainly correct, as it is confirmed in two independent lists in the Kiambu files. But Ngigi he dates as 1892, following Routledge. The period between the circumcision of a man and that of his son is thus in this particular instance sixteen years. Such a short period must be regarded as extremely unlikely in the days before the regimental system had been dislocated. This suggests that the date given by Routledge for Ngigi is several years too late.

It will have been noticed that there were three distinct methods of naming regiments. In one, common in central and southern Kikuyu, the regiment was given an in-dependent name which was not that of any of its sets. In the second, common in northern Kikuyu, the regimental name was normally that of the first set. The third made use of alternating names as well as individual names based usually on the second method. The alternating names were Ndirangu or Mangucha, and so on. These names appear to be the names of previous regiments (three of them occur in the Tetu list), but as the regimental periods were not the same in all the areas in which the alternating names were used they are of little value for the purpose of dating.

Embu

The Embu and Mbere system is based on two principles: that a man's children should be initiated in order of seniority, irrespective of sex, and the generally accepted one that a man must not marry the daughter of a man of his own regiment. As a result of the first principle there could be no closed period for the initiation of boys; a boy must be circumcised before or at the same time as his younger sister, and she must be initiated before the onset of the menses. As a result of the second principle, the men of a suitable age to be acceptable as husbands, *i.e.*, not very much more than ten years older than their brides, must belong to a different regiment from that of the latters' fathers. The grouping of the sets into regiments (*marua*, sing. *irua*) had to be arranged accordingly. This was done, not on any fixed timetable but as the situation might demand, by the tribal elders in consultation. In accordance with the first principle a few boys were circumcised almost every year, but occasionally there would be many male initiates most of whom had reached an age when they would be useful warriors and whose choice of time for circumcision had not depended on the near approach to puberty of younger sisters. Such a large initiation school would be given a specific name and would be considered a *karua*. But it would absorb the initiates of the next few years. The elders say that during a period of twelve years or so there would be two or three *turua*. Some fourteen years after the end of this period some of the older members of the first *karua* would have marriageable daughters, who would be requiring husbands belonging to some *karua* a number of whose members had reached a marriageable age for men, after a reasonable length of front line service as unmarried warriors. This

24 KIKUYU SOCIAL AND POLITICAL INSTITUTIONS

would be most readily provided for by grouping the *turua* into two regiments, from the junior of which the husbands could be chosen. Hence the completion of a regiment must take roughly half as long as the normal period between the circumcision of a man and the initiation (shortly before puberty) of his first-born daughter. If this period be taken as twenty-six years, the average length of time taken to complete a regiment would be thirteen years.

Accordingly the Embu and Mbere grouped together two or three or four *turua* of male initiates, circumcised during a period of thirteen years or thereabouts, into one *irua* which was usually named after its largest *karua*. The system is illustrated in the following table; the dates must be regarded as approximations only. The Gatumo was the last regiment to be formed.

Years	Circumcision Sets	Regiments
1883-7	Mwathamo	
1888-91	Gathuku	MWATHAMO
1892-5	Ngungi ya Mirambua	
1896-9	Gachuthe	
1900-2	Wanjanjagwa	KITHAMBARA
1903-5	Kithambara	
1906-8	Gatego	
1909-12	Kiamatama	
1913-17	Kiamate	GATUMO
1918-21	Gatumo	
1922-4	Rumemo	
1924-34	Ngichiri	
1935 onwards	Njanduru	

The eldest sons of the Mwathamo *karua* belong to

THE REGIMENTAL SYSTEM

Kiamatama and Kiamate, and their eldest grandsons are said by the elders to belong to Njanduru. The eldest daughters of Mwathamo were initiated at the time of the circumcision of the Gatego and Kiamatama *turua*. Most of them married men of the Kithambara regiment. They could not marry men of the Mwathamo regiment.

Various *turua* names other than those listed are sometimes heard. In a few cases these may be merely alternatives, but they generally refer to *turua* which were subsequently absorbed, or to years when only girls were initiated.

The following is the list of regiments in Mbere:

Years	*Circumcision Sets*	*Regiments*
1883-7	Kiobe	
1888-91	Gachuthe	NGUNGI
1892-5	Ngungi ya Itari	
1896-1901	Muviru	
1902-8	Kang'ore	MUVIRU
1909-12	Ngurungu	
1913-17	Mwaranjara	NGURUNGU
1918-21	Wakamuku	
1922-8	Ngichiri	
1929-34	Mbogiro	NGICHIRI

1935 onwards Njanduru

The Mbere elders say that Ngichiri was the last regiment to be formed and that the whole system has now fallen into disuse owing to the virtual demobilization of the warriors and the modern disinclination of youth to be regimented.

The eldest sons of Kiobe are in the Ngurungu regiment

c

26 KIKUYU SOCIAL AND POLITICAL INSTITUTIONS

and their eldest daughters were initiated at the time of the circumcision of Kang'ore and Ngurungu *turua*. They could not marry men of the Ngungi regiment and if the latter had been extended to include the Muviru *karua* those girls (daughters of Kiobe) who first attained nubility would have been restricted in their choice of youngish husbands to Kang'ore, who were initiated at much the same time as themselves. The military system would then have been in danger of disruption.

Meru

In the Meru group, including Miutini, Igoji, Mwimbi, Muthambi and Tharaka, the word for the named group of young men circumcised within a limited period, which I have called a regiment, was *nthuki*. The *nthuki* period is stated by the elders to have been ten years or so, though in fact it is much longer. In Tigania and Igembe there are three circumcisions, and in the rest two during this period, and each separate set has its own name also. Apart from its individual name, each set has an ordinal name; these names are the same for every *nthuki*. In Tigania and Igembe the first group is called Ndinguri, the middle group Kobia, and the last group Kaberia. In Imenti and the rest the senior group is called Chankanabiri and the junior group Ntimirigwe or Nturutimi. This arrangement is illustrated in the following tables:

TIGANIA AND IGEMBE

Ordinal Names	Sets of Kiramunya	Sets of Itharie
1. Ndinguri	Kiraithe	Kiambarua
2. Kobia	Kirianki	Mithiga (Munjuri)
3. Kaberia	Kirungi (Ntarangwi)	Muthimu (Ntabatia)

THE REGIMENTAL SYSTEM 27

IMENTI

Ordinal Names	Sets of Murungi	Sets of Miriti
1. Chankanabiri	Riungu	Ntarangwi
2. Ntimirigwe	Kirianki	Nkonge

In some instances the Meru offer meanings of the ordinal names in explanation of their use. Thus *ndinguri* is said to mean 'those who have waited a long time' and the word is sometimes applied to youths about to be circumcised, irrespective of what their order will be in their set. It was formerly particularly applied to over-grown youths who, if age were the only consideration, would have been circumcised some time before. They were often young men who had been prevented by some circumstance, such as a death in the family, from being circumcised with youths of their own age.

Theoretically the Mwimbi follow the Imenti system. But in practice they often have three sets with distinctive names in each *nthuki*. The third is then sometimes called *mwongera*, 'the increase'. It often forms the nucleus of the first set of the next *nthuki* as well as the last of its own. This creates some degree of overlapping as between Mwimbi and Imenti and in Mwimbi itself a less clear-cut distinction between succeeding sets than that in Meru proper.

It seems possible that the three-set system was the original one and that theoretically the period between the start of one set and the next was seven clear seasons, no male circumcision occurring in the seventh; so that the time occupied in the formation of a complete *nthuki* was twenty-four seasons, that is, about twelve years. In Imenti there were sometimes as many as five circumcision sets in the

28 KIKUYU SOCIAL AND POLITICAL INSTITUTIONS

nthuki, but these were joined up into two with special names.[1]

We shall take Laughton's carefully compiled list[2] of *nthuki* as the basis for comparison with other Imenti lists. The Rev. A. J. Hopkins prepared a list for the District Commissioner, Meru, in May 1924; it starts with Mukuruma, which, according to his informant, was the first *nthuki* to be circumcised in the present Meru country. These two lists, taken respectively from Laughton's monograph and the Meru political record, are compared with a composite list made up from information supplied more recently by numerous elders:

Hopkins (1924)	Laughton (1938)	1944
		[1. Kibiringwa]
		[2. Mujogo]
	1. Ntangi	3. Ntangi
	2. Nkuthuku	4. Nkuthuku
1. Mukuruma	3. Mukuruma	5. Mukuruma
2. Kitharie	4. Githarie	6. Mbaine
3. Michubu	5. Michubu	7. Michugu
4. Latanya	6. Latanya	8. Ratanya
5. Thangiria	7. Githangiria	9. Githangiria
6. Mbaringo	8. Mbaringo	10. Mbaringo
7. Nkuthugwa	9. Nguthogua	11. Nguthugua
8. Mbarata	10. Mbarata	12. Mbarata
9. Kiruja	11. Kiruja	13. Kiruja
10. Thamburu	12. Thamburu	14. Thamburu
11. Nangithia	13. Nturutimi	15. Nturutimi
12. Kubai	14. Kubai	16. Kubai
13. Mungatia	15. Kaburia	17. Kaburia
14. Memeu	16. Kiramana	18. Kiriamana
15. Murungi	17. Murungi	19. Murungi
16. Ntarangwi	18. Miriti	20. Miriti
	19. Kiruja	21. Kiruja
	20. Gwantai	22. Gwantai

[1] In Imenti a third sub-set name was sometimes used temporarily, e.g. Miriti consisted of Ntarangwi, Kaburu, and Nkonge during its warrior days.

[2] Based on a list supplied by the Rev. P. M'Inoti and filed in the Meru Political Record.

THE REGIMENTAL SYSTEM 29

Apart from a few differences in naming these lists are in complete accord, though informants nowadays sometimes give a slightly different order for the earlier period. In the case of three of the instances where names differ, it is possible to identify with certainty the *nthuki* represented by the different names. Mungatia (Mung'athia) is the name of the Chankanabiri set of Kaburia, so that the *nthuki* which is named Mungatia in the Hopkins list is that called Kaburia in the other two. Similarly Memeu is the Chankanabiri set of Kiramana; the two names in fact are interchangeable, Kiramana being sometimes given as the Chankanabiri set of the Memeu. Ntarangwi is the Chankanabiri set of Miriti and this was the only set following Murungi which had been formed at the time the Hopkins list was compiled.

The Tigania names differ from those used in Imenti, but the correspondences are exact and the more recent ones are known precisely. The Igembe naming is the same as that of Tigania.

Theoretically the Mwimbi follow the Imenti system and the Imenti naming. But names rarely, if ever, heard in Imenti occasionally occur in Mwimbi lists and the names of sets in Imenti are sometimes used as alternative names for *nthuki* in Mwimbi. Though the system is essentially the same, Mwimbi appears to have got 'out of step' with Imenti to a considerable extent, more particularly in recent years. It seems that circumcisions took place at approximately the same time in both sub-tribes, but the amalgamation of sets was somewhat different. It is possible that the separation of the two sub-tribes caused by administration from two different District headquarters tended to reduce the usual liaison, but even before this there was far less emphasis in the Mwimbi system on the demarcation of the boundary between two sets, that is to

30 KIKUYU SOCIAL AND POLITICAL INSTITUTIONS

say, less emphasis on the artificial generation. The following comparison between the two illustrates the lack of accord in the building up of *nthuki*. The Mwimbi list was given me by a Mwimbi elder in 1932, before the two sub-tribes had been put into one administrative district.

IMENTI		MWIMBI	
Sets	*Nthuki*	*Sets*	*Nthuki*
Gwantai / Miriti	Thamburu	Ragu / Thamburu / Mucheu	Thamburu
Kobia / Kibabu	Nturutimi	Kobia / Kibabu / Nturutimi	Kobia
Kang'ethe / Gichungi	Kubai	Kubai / Gichungi / Kaburia	Kaburia
Mung'athia / Kamundi	Kaburia	Nchunuku / Muringi / Kibai	Kamundi
Memeu / Kiambobwa	Kiramana	Kiriamana / Kiriambobwa / Kiraithe	Murungi
Riungu / Kirianki	Murungi	Riungu / Marangu / Kirianki	Kirianki
Ntarangwi / Nkonge	Miriti	Ntarangwi / Kaburu / Nkonge	Miriti

Since the two sub-tribes began to be administered together (1933) and the tribal organization has been recognized and used by Government, there has been an attempt to 'get into step' again and Mwimbi

THE REGIMENTAL SYSTEM

lists of sets now correspond to Imenti ones, though there is some difference in the actual naming most commonly used.

Theoretically, the Tharaka also take their set names from Imenti, but there is sometimes a time-lag and the name may be that of a young set of a preceding Imenti *nthuki* or of the Imenti set next in order.

4

PRE-INITIATION AGE-SETS

Boys who are approaching the age for circumcision form bands for sports, hunting and frequently mischief. These bands have names, which may be either newly invented or taken from those of earlier bands; in the latter case the name taken is that of the corresponding band in the age-set to which they stand in filial relationship.

In Kikuyu the division of children into sets applies strictly speaking only to boys, but small girls of corresponding age are included in a set unless the context naturally excludes them. There appear to have been both generic and specific names for these pre-initiation sets, but nowadays the emphasis in northern Kikuyu is on the former and in central and southern Kikuyu on the latter. The generic names are Kabichu for the small boys' set, Njoya for those of intermediate age, and Murichu (or its collective form, Ndichu) for those approaching circumcision age, including the *ihii chia muhiiro* ('lads of the blossoming') who are decorated for the pre-initiation dances. In northern Gaki, Murichu or Ndichu is very rarely used of pre-initiates, but the elders liken the three divisions of boys to the three grades of initiated warriors, the oldest corresponding to the *aanake*, of whom the first set in every group of sets is known as Murichu, the second set (Njoya) to the *mumo* (recently established warriors, who are sometimes called Njoya), and the third (Kabichu) to the *chiumiri* (neophytes). In southern Kikuyu, on both sides of the Chania river, generic names are rarely heard,

PRE-INITIATION AGE-SETS

though Njoya and Ndichu sometimes occur as though they were specific names.

In many places only two sets are recognized, and the youngest boys, who are scarcely old enough for communal activities, have no name at all. The names vary to some extent from place to place. They are often those of earlier initiation sets. There is no formality about the system and alternatives are not infrequent. The boys of a pre-initiation set are not necessarily all initiated together; some may be delayed by illness or a local shortage of food. Thus, if one asks two men of the same locality, who belong to the same initiation set, what their set was called before it was initiated, one may get a different name from each. The following names cannot therefore be taken as applicable to every member of the initiation set to which reference is made.

Men who became, about 1885, the Ngigi ('locusts') initiation set had been known in middle childhood as Kiburi and just prior to initiation as Mjinga. Similarly men who became, about 1890, the Mutung'u ('smallpox') set had been known successively as Gatiti and Njegegu. A majority of the Kienjeku ('scores') set (about 1894) had been known as Ndichu when they were well-grown lads and previously as Kiboko. One elder gave their 'baby name' as Mwichaga. Coming to more recent times, a man of the Chiringi ('shilling') set, initiated about 1923, gave as his pre-initiation sets first Mirianda, then Mbuku and then, just before initiation, Chaki. Another Chiringi gave Gachutha and Mbuku and had not heard of Chaki.

One of the names of a man's pre-initiation set is sometimes given as a nickname (the individual as distinct from the 'inherited' name) to a child (a grandson or a nephew) named after him.

Though the division into pre-initiation sets applies

34 KIKUYU SOCIAL AND POLITICAL INSTITUTIONS

particularly to boys, girls of a similar age are colloquially included and have the same set names applied to them. On initiation the youths and girls become *chiumiri* ('those who come out', neophytes) and receive their final age-set name which the set retains through life. Since girls are initiated before they begin to menstruate (*ona mugongo wa mbere*, 'see the first back', or *ona mweri hingo ya mbere*, 'see the moon for the first time'), they generally belong to final sets the boys of which are older than they are by several years.

In a sense it may be said that there is a division of young people into non-sexual groups up to the time when sex attraction is socially recognized as quite properly an active influence on behaviour. Children born at approximately the same time belong successively to the asexual groups (that is, groups undifferentiated sexually by name) of *tukenge* (babies), *twana* (infants), then two or three named sets, then *chiumiri* (neophytes), and then *mumo* (young adults). Girls do not have age sets in the strict sense, but names which correspond to those taken by the boys are used to indicate girls of comparable age; owing to the earlier age of initiation for girls, they may belong to only one or two named groups. The final preparation for a functional differentiation by sex occurs at circumcision, but even then the boy or girl belongs to the asexual group called *chiumiri* until he or she has undergone a ceremony to which the stem *thiga* is applied. The word *guthiga* implies entry into adult life, and nowadays is sometimes used to denote adultery, no doubt because the ceremony used to include a sexual act which in other circumstances would be contrary to law. After this ceremony both boys and girls are called *mumo* until they have paid the appropriate fees to their seniors and received instruction in the rules of the limited sexual activity permitted to the next

PRE-INITIATION AGE-SETS

grade, at which for the first time the sexes are differentiated, boys becoming *aanake* and girls *airitu*. The *mumo* boys may be regarded loosely as recruits or freshmen, the *mumo* girls as debutantes.

The organization of pre-initiation sets reaches its greatest elaboration among the Meru proper (Imenti, Tigania and Igembe), where a formal grading is recognized all through a sub-tribe and not uncommonly through all the sub-tribes. The following tables give the names for recent pre-initiation sets in the three sub-tribes:

(a) IMENTI

Ordinal Name	Pre-Initiation Name of Set	Initiation Name of Set
	KIRAMANA	
Chankanabiri	Karemu	Memeu (Kiramana)
Ntimirigwe	Mwengirua	Kiambobwa
	MURUNGI	
Chankanabiri	Mwiraria (Raria)	Riungu
Ntimirigwe	Kanyagia	Kirianki
	MIRITI	
Chankanabiri	Muthaura	Ntarangwi
Ntimirigwe	Muriira	Nkonge
	KIRUJA	
Chankanabiri	Muthiora	Kaburu
Ntimirigwe	Mwongera	Gichuru
	GWANTAI	
Chankanabiri	Muthaura	Kimonye
Ntimirigwe	Muriira	Mbaya (Kibaya)

(b) TIGANIA AND IGEMBE

Ordinal Name	Pre-Initiation Name of Set		Initiation Name of Set
	GICHUNGI		
	Tigania	Igembe	
Ndinguri	Muriira	Muriira	Gichungi
Kobia	Mwanjati	Mwanjati	Gichunuku
Kaberia	Mwengirua	Mwengirua	Kiramana

36 KIKUYU SOCIAL AND POLITICAL INSTITUTIONS

KIRAMUNYA

Ndinguri	Mwiraria	Rimiri	Kiraithe
Kobia	Kiremi	Mwiraria	Kirianki
Kaberia	Muthaura	Mwongera	Kirungi

ITHARIE

Ndinguri	Muriira	Muriira	Kiambarua
Kobia	Mwanjati	Mwanjati	Mithiga (Munjuri)
Kaberia	Mwengirua	Kiremi (?)	Muthimu (Ntabatia)

MICHUBU

Ndinguri	Rimiri	Rimiri	Michubu
Kobia	Kiremi	Kiremi	Mwithirua
Kaberia	Muthaura	Muthaura	Murikinyi

I have given no names for the sets following Michubu because they do not yet appear to be generally agreed upon. There was some dislocation some eleven or twelve years ago (1934 and 1935) owing to the fact that it was considered necessary in Tigania and Igembe to 'clear the way' for the initiation of *nkenye* (uncircumcised girls) by first initiating the *biiji* (uncircumcised lads). This is reflected in the fact that the pre-initiation set called Muthaura here became the Kaberia set of Michubu, whereas in Imenti it became the Chankanabiri set of the following set (Gwantai). A similar thing had happened some twenty-five or twenty-six years before, possibly for the same reason. Members of pre-initiation sub-sets do not necessarily belong to the same sub-sets after initiation, since some boys' initiation is usually postponed for one reason or another.

Girls' Sets. In the sub-tribes in which the final initiation of girls (clitoridectomy) is not performed till marriage, girls form similar pre-initiation sets. Girls of approximately the same age, who work together at various communal occupations (*ngugi*), give themselves a name which generally comes into universal use to denote all girls of a like age throughout the sub-tribe. When these girls

PRE-INITIATION AGE-SETS

arrive at sexual maturity, as indicated by a noticeable development of the breasts and by the fact that they desire a sexual intercourse more complete than the minor sex-play indulged in by children, they are permitted to practise a limited coition with the initiated unmarried men who are the warriors at that time, and from among whom their husbands will normally come, and they are described collectively as the *nkenye* (girls) *cha buuru* of the warrior sets in question. *Buuru* means 'friendship', or 'set' in the sense of such expressions as 'the younger set' or 'the right set', a group of persons who for some reason or purpose naturally hold together. The word can also be used of the warriors of a particular locality. When the members of a man's sub-set name their *nkenye cha buuru* they mean the girls' set to which their lovers belong (or did belong), and to which their first wives will have belonged (or did belong) as long as they (the wives) are (or were) uninitiated; in fact a considerable number of the girls so described are debarred from sex relations with any given man of the set, since marriage prohibitions apply equally to pre-marital intercourse.

The following lists indicate the correspondences between male and female sub-sets:

(a) IMENTI

Men: KIRAMANA		*Women:* NCHOROBI
Ordinal Name	*Men's Set*	*Girl's Set*
Chankanabiri	Memeu	Nchekei
Ntimirigwe	Kiambobwa	Ntibuka
Men: MURUNGI		*Women:* THIRINDI
Chankanabiri	Riungu	Karegi
Ntimirigwe	Kirianki	Regeria
Men: MIRITI		*Women:* NCHECHENGA
Chankanabiri	Ntarangwi	Nyoroka
Ntimirigwe	Nkonge	Kibuto

38 KIKUYU SOCIAL AND POLITICAL INSTITUTIONS

Men: KIRUJA		Women: Not yet named
Chankanabiri	Kaburu	Nchekei
Ntimirigwe	Gichuru	Rigiri (Nyegera)

The only girls' set I have heard named as the *nkenye cha buuru* of the Gwantai set is Nyegera. There was an unusually rapid initiation of the girls at the time Gwantai was in process of formation. There were accordingly plenty of *ngutu* but few *nkenye* and Gichuru shared Nyegera with Gwantai. This was no doubt against Gichuru's will and Nyegera is consequently said to be Gichuru's set of *nkenye cha buuru* with the rider added, 'stolen by Gwantai'.

The married women's set Nchechenga is also called Mucheche.

(*b*) TIGANIA

Ordinal Name	Men: GICHUNGI	Women: NCHOROBI
Ndinguri	Muriira	Thirigwa
Kobia	Mwanjati	Kiburo
Kaberia	Mwengirua	Munyaki
	Men: KIRAMUNYA	Women: THIRINDI
Ndinguri	Mwiraria	Riiri
Kobia	Kiremi	Karei
Kaberia	Muthaura	Reeria
	Men: ITHARIE	Women: NCHORORO
Ndinguri	Muriira	Nyoroka
Kobia	Mwanjati	Thirigwa
Kaberia	Mwengirua	Munyata
	Men: MICHUBU	Women: (MUKUBU)
Ndinguri	Rimiri	Thairora
Kobia	Kiremi	Not named?
Kaberia	Muthaura	Not named?

The women who married Michubu are known as Mukubu, but they have not yet been formally named.

The *nkenye cha buuru* of the Kobia and Kaberia sets of Michubu apparently went unnamed, the majority having been initiated before the usual age.

PRE-INITIATION AGE-SETS

(c) IGEMBE

Ordinal Name	Men: GICHUNGI	Women: NCHOROBI
Ndinguri	Muriira	Nkaithiori
Kobia	Mwanjati	Kiburo
Kaberia	Mwengirua	Munyaki
	Men: KIRAMUNYA	Women: THIRINDI
Ndinguri	Rimiri	Riiri
Kobia	Mwiraria	Karei
Kaberia	Mwongera	Karuta
	Men: ITHARIE	Women: NCHORORO
Ndinguri	Muriira	Nyoroka
Kobia	Mwanjati	Thirigwa
Kaberia	Kiremi (?)	Munyata
	Men: MICHUBU	Women: Not yet named
Ndinguri	Rimiri	Nkairora
Kobia	Kiremi	Not named?
Kaberia	Muthaura	Not named?

Normally men marry as their first wives girls who are *nkenye cha buuru* of their post-initiation set, so that the majority of the first wives of a set are of the same pre-initiation set of girls, and a woman's set consists of the first wives of a man's *nthuki* and receives its name when the men's *nthuki* receives its final name, that is at the *ntuiko* ceremony. But the name of the women's set is in practice frequently extended to include all the wives of the men of one *nthuki*.

5

THE GENERATION[1]

In all tribes of the unit political authority at any given time is held to be vested in the elders of one generation. The accession of a new generation to power takes place at regular intervals and is formally signalized by the handing over ceremony (Kikuyu *ituiko*, Meru *ntuiko*). The Kikuyu mode of reckoning the generations is the simplest: among some other tribes a complication is introduced by the division of the population into two sections whose generations overlap.

The common term for a generation in Kikuyu is *riika* (pl. *mariika*), though when biological relationships are stressed *ruchiaro* (pl. *njiaro*) or *njiarua* (pl. *njiarua*) may be used. Every generation inherits the name of that to which its grandfather belonged, though this is normally only applied to it when it is politically immature, that is before it had become the ruling generation designate. Thus there is a perpetual alternation of two names. The ruling generation may be distinguished from that of its grandsons by a prefix or qualifying phrase.

A second name indicates its position in a cycle. It must be remarked, however, that the existence of a generation cycle does not appear to be recognized by the majority of elders, and I do not feel any confidence with regard to the cycle in central and southern Kikuyu. Nevertheless I think that the available evidence, which I hope to present

---

[1] This subject is treated briefly, as I hope to present further material on it elsewhere.

THE GENERATION

elsewhere, points to the existence of a seven-generation
cycle in Gichugu and Ndia and the northern part of Gaki
and, though with less certainty, to an eight-generation
cycle in central and southern Kikuyu. Leakey, in a
hitherto unpublished study of the southern Kikuyu, de-
scribes a cycle of nine generations.

Meanwhile, I tentatively record the northern Kikuyu
cycle as follows:

While two Generations Younger than the Ruling Generation	While One Generation Younger than the Ruling Generation	While Ruling
1. Kamwangi	Chuma Kaguku	Chuma
2. Kairungu	Mathathi Kaguku	Mathathi
3. Gachuma	Ndemi Kaguku	Ndemi
4. Kamathathi	Iregi Kaguku	Iregi
5. Kandemi	Maina Kaguku	Maina
6. Kairegi	Mwangi Kaguku	Mwangi
7. Kamaina	Irungu Kaguku	Irungu
1. Kamwangi	Chuma Kaguku	Chuma

The third name that a generation cycle gets is its
individual name. But with recent generations there is no
clear-cut distinction between cyclical and individual
names. Indeed there is nothing to show that there ever
were cyclical names which were not in some cycle or other
the individual names of generations.

The practical determination of the period of a generation depends on the apparent composition of society at
the time. When most of the first-born grandsons of the
ruling generation have been circumcised it is felt that
the time is approaching for that generation to relinquish
rule, so that normally the gap between two official
generations is much the same as the gap between the

D

42 KIKUYU SOCIAL AND POLITICAL INSTITUTIONS

average ages of a man and his first-born son. In Fort Hall the general opinion seems to be that thirty years is too low. The Beechers in their dictionary record that—

The Maina generation handed over to the Mwangi grade at the end of the last century and they in turn began to hand over to the Irungu in 1931-2. The handing-over ceremony takes years to complete.

This, with other evidence quoted by Hobley and derived from the Fort Hall Political Record, tends to confirm a gap of about thirty years.

In Embu, Mbere and Chuka the word for a generation in the political sense is *nduki* or *nthuki*. The whole population is grouped in two divisions whose generation periods overlap, so that the taking over occurs at a different date in each. These sections are usually known in Embu as Kimanthi and Nyangi, in Mbere as Kimanthi (or Thathi) and Nyangi, and in Chuka as Thathi and Nyangi. In Embu and Mbere the last taking over in the Kamanthi division was in 1932 and the last in the Nyangi division in about 1925; this was delayed by the 1914-18 War and by the opposition of government officials. In Chuka Thathi took over in 1948 and Nyangi in 1945. Normally a man belongs to the filial generation of his father's generation and each succeeding generation is the equivalent, or the repetition, of its grandfather generation. The sons of a man in one division, however, could sometimes be transferred into the other.

The division into two is said by the Embu to have occurred in the generation called Kubai, but they are not quite clear whether this refers to a generation of the Kimanthi division called Kubai some four generations ago or to Kubai Kuraja, 'distant Kubai', which occurred very

THE GENERATION 43

much earlier. The tradition is that in the generation preceding Kubai there was a severe famine, named Mbaraganu, which killed off thousands of people, and that Kubai consequently split into two so that at least a moiety of the tribe would remain alive if a similar disaster occurred again. This is in accordance with African ideas, and the principle of 'not putting all one's eggs in one basket' is given by the Embu as the reason why a man sometimes transfers one son or more to the other political division. The generation in which the famine occurred was called Iria and the famine is known as Ng'aragu ya Iria Kuraja ('the famine of the distant Iria') as well as Mbaraganu. It seems probable that it actually happened in the Iria generation, which assumed office in or about A.D. 1810 and 'ruled' till 1840 or thereabouts; one of my informants, of the Kimanthi generation, said that it took place in the time of his great-great-grandfather, which puts it in this generation, and the Tharaka refer to a great famine, which they call Muraja, which happened, they say, during the 'rule' of the Mbarata circumcision age, which, making some allowance for delays, was in power about a hundred and twenty years ago, say about A.D. 1825. But though the famine probably occurred about that time the split, if there ever was one, must have taken place a good deal earlier, for the other division carries its distinctive names back beyond the Iria generation; this, however, is not conclusive, because those more distant generations bear the same names as recent ones and the principle of alternation may account for a belief in their historical existence; they may, in fact, be merely guesswork.

The occurrence of Kikuyu generation-names in the early Tharaka grades suggests some close relationship between the pre-Kikuyu and the pre-Tharaka or the Thaichu.

44 KIKUYU SOCIAL AND POLITICAL INSTITUTIONS

The Chuka themselves volunteer no explanation of their division into two. They refer, however, to a very severe famine, called Rungura, which occurred during the 'rule' of the generations known as Thura and Matumo, in which even the Ruguti and Thuchi rivers were reduced to a few puddles. Many Chuka, it is said, sought refuge in Kikuyu (Ndia) during this famine. About this time the Thura generation of the Nyangi handed over to the Njuki and during the famine they persuaded the Matumo generation of the Thathi to hand over to their filial generation (the Ikuthi) much earlier than they would normally have done, in order to avert disaster. This hand-over was followed by very heavy October rains, remembered as the Nyaga wa Riunga, which flooded all the lower countryside. The Ikuthi had sacrificed for rain and it is still the practice for the Thathi division to sacrifice for the October rains and the Nyangi division for the March rains.

Having regard to the number of generations involved, it seems probable that the Rungura famine of the Chuka was the same as that called Mbaragani by the Embu. This gives us the tentative approximate dating, 1825, for the taking over of the Ikuthi from the Matumo generation, and of the Njuki from the Thura. Thereafter the sequence in the Nyangi division appears to have been more or less normal, while that in the Thathi division was somewhat dislocated by the early taking over of Ikuthi and again by the 1939-45 War.

It is rare to meet an elder in Embu or Mbere who can name more than four or five generations, though individual elders can often name twice as many ancestors in the patrilineal line. The following list gives the Embu generations (for each division) of which any clear traditional memory was retained by my informants. The

THE GENERATION

45

approximate date of 'taking over' is shown against each.

EMBU

Kimanthi Division		*Nyangi Division*	
A.D.		A.D.	
1782	1. Maithi	1768	1. Muranja
1812	2. Iria	1798	2. Nyangi
1842	3. Kubai	1828	3. Riyuu
1872	4. Kinyare	1858	4. Karara
1902	5. Irungu (Ndure)	1888	5. Muranja (Merambu)
1932	6. Kimanthi (Ndiiriri)	1925	6. Nyangi (Thume)
	7. Kanyakamburi (Mwita)		

The alternating names based on the substantive identification of a generation with its 'grandfather' and 'grandson' generations, are Kimanthi and Irungu in the one division and Nyangi and Merambu in the other. Though every generation has its special name these alternations are frequently emphasized by the use of 'small' (recent) and 'great' (old); thus Irungu Inyinyi distinguishes the recent Irungu from Kubai, which may be referred to as Irungu Nguru; Nyangi Nguru is Karara. Kuraja ('a long way off') is sometimes used to indicate remoteness in the alternation; there is some suggestion of a recurring cycle in the use of this word, Kubai Kuraja, for instance, appearing at times to refer to the generation called Kubai not in the present list but in an earlier cycle similarly named; it seems that the cycle may consist of seven generations, but my informants could not be definite on the point; if there ever was a cycle it has been thoroughly obscured by alternation.

The more recent Mbere generations are as follows:

46 KIKUYU SOCIAL AND POLITICAL INSTITUTIONS

Thathi Division	Nyangi Division
A.D.	A.D.
1782 1. Githandika	1768 1. ?
1812 2. Thathi Nguru	1798 2. Nyangi Nguru
1842 3. Mukunga	1828 3. Ndaugi Nguru
1872 4. Kinyare	1858 4. Mbiriga
1902 5. Ndure	1888 5. Kinogu
1932 6. Thathi	1918 6. Nyangi
	7. Ndaugi or Ivate

The alternations are referred to nowadays as Thathi and Kinyare in the one division and Nyangi and Ndaugi in the other, though the Embu names are sometimes used instead. The *g* of Ndaugi is frequently reduced almost to inaudibility, as it would be in Kamba.

In Chuka even fewer generation names are generally remembered than in Embu and Mbere. The Chuka say that this is due to the widespread dislocation caused by raids. However that may be, it seems quite certain that the Chuka, broken from time to time into bands of terror-stricken fugitives during a period of possibly a hundred years, had little heart or opportunity for the formal gatherings essential to their theory of tribal constitution. For this reason it is more than likely that the tentative dates given in the following list of the Chuka generations should be spaced more widely, that, for instance, Mbai, which is of the Nyangi alternation and claims to be ruling now (1946), has not completely taken over and that forty years was the average length of 'rule' from Njuki onwards.

Thathi Division	Nyangi Division
A.D.	A.D.
1810 1. Matumo	1795 1. Thura
1825 2. Ikuthi	1825 2. Njuki
1870 3. Nthithuki	1855 3. Mwichuki
1905 4. Ndigia	1885 4. Ntatua
(1948) 5. (Thathi)	1915 5. (Nyangi Mbai)
	(1945) 6. (Ntatua)

THE GENERATION

The alternating names are Thathi and Ndigia in the one division and Nyangi and Ntatua in the other. The name Nthithuki has a dialectal variant Mbithuki.

It appears that the choice of the names for the generations at the various stages rests with one family of the Igamuturi clan, who are said also to exercise a general direction of the whole proceedings. No doubt we can see in this, as also in the account of the Kikuyu handing-over, some hereditary function vested in a kinship group or groups, rather like the *ugwe* of the Meru.

The Chuka, like the Embu and Mbere, have several sacred groves for each division, but those considered by the tribe to be the most important of the sacred places are Igambang'ombe for the Thathi and Mwenjeu for the Nyangi.

In Meru there is no grouping of regiments into generations: the word *nthuki* denotes a single group of initiation sets, and it is these groups which alternate. The alternating names are Kiruka and Ntiba: in Tigania and Igembe the latter is often called Gitiba. The relation between them is illustrated in the following table, which works backwards from the present warrior set:

KIRUKA	NTIBA
Gwantai	Kiruja
Miriti	Murungi
Kiramana	Kaburia
Kubai	
etc.	etc.

The political status of the two divisions from 1941 was as follows:

KIRUKA	NTIBA
Warriors	Young married men
Ruling set	ex-Ruling set

48 KIKUYU SOCIAL AND POLITICAL INSTITUTIONS

At the next *ntuiko* the position will be reversed, Kiruka containing the young married men and the ex-Ruling set and Ntiba the Warriors and the Ruling set. All that 'ruling' in this respect infers is that officially the country is in the charge of the set called 'ruling set' and that it is the Warriors, who are in the same division, who form the first line of defence. This is frequently expressed by natives in the form "The country now belongs to Kiruka; when Kiruja takes over from Miriti it will belong to Ntiba," by which they mean: "The care of the country is now primarily in the hands of Kiruka; this duty will become Ntiba's when Kiruja takes over from Miriti."

The relationship between *nthuki* is described in terms of descent. For example, Kiramana, who are now aged men, speak of Miriti as 'our sons' and of Gwantai as 'our grandsons'. This usage is, of course, metaphorical: in fact a majority of their actual sons are in Kiruja, while most of their actual grandsons do not yet belong to any *nthuki*.

Eight *nthuki*, four Kiruka and four Ntiba form a cycle. This is not very obvious from any list of sets and, as is the case in Kikuyu, the elders do not volunteer any information about it and indeed do not appear to realize that there is a cycle at all, though they readily agree that there is one as soon as it is pointed out to them. Its existence is obscured by the common use of individual rather than cyclical names for sets, and it is in fact impossible to determine which, if any, of the names listed are cyclical. But that there is a cycle (suggested by the recurrence of Kiruja in Imenti, by the fact that the Murungi sometimes call themselves Nguthugua, and by the recurrence of Michubu and Elatanya in Tigania) becomes clear when one asks what names the 'sons' of recent sets will have.

THE GENERATION 49

The answer is always: "We do not know what their name will be. That is a matter for the *mugwe* at the time of the *ntuiko*. But they will certainly be So-and-So". Thus in Imenti the sets filial to Kiruja and Gwantai will, the elders say, be Nturutimi and Kubai respectively, though they may be given individual names when their 'fathers' assume the rule and still further names when they themselves assume it. The Tigania elders say that the present warriors, that is the set following Michubu, "are not yet named, but they are Elatanya and their sons will be Miriti".

If we use the most commonly recurring names as far as possible as cyclical we can record the Meru cycles thus:

TIGANIA AND IGEMBE

Gitiba (Ntiba)	*Kiruka*
1. Michubu	2. Elatanya
3. Elubetaa	4. Miriti
5. Gwantai	6. Gichungi
7. Mbaine	8. Itharie

IMENTI, ETC.

1. Kiruja	2. Itharie (Gwantai) (Mbaine)
3. Michubu	4. Latanya
5. Githangiria (Kaburia)	6. Kiramana
7. Nguthugua	8. Miriti

There are some curious similarities and differences between these two sub-tribal cycles. The sequence Itharie-Michubu-Latanya occurs in both, but starts one artificial generation later in Imenti than in Tigania. Imenti has Kiruja between Miriti and Gwantai, so that these two are of the same political division (Kiruka), whereas in Tigania they are of different divisions. This difference would be expressed by the Meru in the statement that in Imenti Gwantai are Miriti's sons but in

50 KIKUYU SOCIAL AND POLITICAL INSTITUTIONS

Tigania they are Miriti's younger brothers. I could get no explanation of these discrepancies from any of the elders; I am satisfied that they are not due to any mis-recording of the cycles, though I am not sure about the position of Mbaine in Imenti.[1]

Asked to express the relationship between sets holding similar positions in two successive cycles the elders say that the earlier consists of the *ba nguku* or *ba kichukuru* of the later; thus a man of the recent Miriti in Imenti would say *Mbarata ii bangukui* 'Mbarata are my ancestors'. But these expressions merely mean 'distant ancestors' or when used with more precision 'great-great-grandfathers' and do not in themselves imply a cycle. The various terms in common use for 'ancestors' are certainly too vague to indicate the length of cycle; thus *Mbarata ni nguku cha Miriti* can be taken to denote the distance in generations between Mbarata and Miriti and given its precise meaning, happens to indicate the correct distance in the sequence, but a Meru is just as likely to say *Mbarata ni ijujui bia Miriti*, which, taken precisely, makes the number of generations one too few, *kijujui* meaning 'great-grand-father' or simply 'ancestor', according to the context. An Imenti Miriti man, pressed to be exact, will refer to the Kiramana as *ba baba*, to the Kubai as *ba juju*, to the Thamburu as *ba kijuju* and to the Mbarata as *ba kichukuru* or *bangukui*, but these phrases merely indicate increasing distances in ancestry and do not necessarily stop at Mbarata or imply that Miriti is regarded as a repetition of it in a later cycle. But if Kiramana had been asked to name their 'sons', even before any of the latter had been born, they would certainly have answered: "We don't

---

[1] If, as is quite likely, the early Mbaine of Imenti, Mirimbi and Tharaka has been placed one set too late and should be equated with Kiruja there is the sequence Mbaine-Itharie-Michubu-Latanya in both sub-tribal cycles.

THE GENERATION

know what their name will be but they will be Mbarata".

The married women's sets run similarly in a cycle of eight. Whatever the cyclical names may have indicated originally they now correspond precisely to the sets of the men they marry, that is to say, a woman's set name depends on the set of the man she marries, not on the time of her own initiation. In the case of first wives, however, the majority of the men of a set marry during a period of a few years, and as women's initiation is a pre-nuptial rite the set names of first wives do indicate the period during which the majority were initiated. The following are the cycles of women's sets corresponding to those given above for men's sets. The correspondence indicates marriage. Thus No. 1 (Muthai) are the wives of No. 1 (Michubu) in Tigania.

TIGANIA AND IGEMBE

1. Muthai	2. (Nchechenga)
3. Nkinathi	4. Nkoiyai
5. Nkoroi	6. Nchorobi
7. Thirindi	8. Nchechenga (Nchororo)

IMENTI, ETC.

1. Muthai	2. (Nchechenga)
3. Nkirinathi	4. Nkoiyai
5. Munyange	6. Nchorobi
7. Thirindi	8. Nchechenga (Mucheche)

I have put No. 2 (Nchechenga) in brackets because this name also appears as No. 8. But it was the only name for No. 2 that I could get from my informants. If it is correct it means that the wives of the 'sons' (Gwantai) of Miriti in Imenti, for instance, will have the same cyclical name as the wives of Miriti, which seems unlikely.

52 KIKUYU SOCIAL AND POLITICAL INSTITUTIONS

It will be noticed that there is a closer similarity between the cyclical names of women's set in the two groups of sub-tribes than between those of the men. No. 8 of Tigania (men) has the same name as No. 2 of Imenti. Some confusion arising from this fact may account for the apparent repetition of Mchechenga in the women's cycle.

6

RITUALS OF THE AGE ORGANIZATION

THE appropriate season for circumcision was in the warm, dry weather (*themithu*) after the millet harvest in February. But frequently circumcisions were still in progress in April or even May, after the break of the long rains (*mbura ya njihi*, 'rain of the dolichos beans').

It was followed by the *guthiga* ceremony, the essential features of which were a partial shaving of the head, the smearing of red ochre (*thiriga*) on the head and body, and the change of clothing, boys now wearing warriors' cloaks and the girls the long-tailed type of skirt. But in the Kikuyu guild the boys had formerly to perform the act of ceremonial rape called *kuihaka muunya* (to smear oneself with salt earth). According to some accounts, this had to take place before the *guthiga* itself, according to others after it. The male *chiumiri* of the Kikuyu guild wandered the countryside in bands, usually well away from their homes. The object of each band was to find a woman, who must be of married status and a stranger to them, on whom to commit the rape. The ideal woman would be of the Kamba tribe, which was persistently at enmity with the Kikuyu wherever the tribes were fairly near to one another, but failing a Kamba or other foreign woman a Kikuyu from a distant area would serve. In theory every youth in the band (there might be as many as a hundred at times, according to the elders) had to *ihaka muunyu* by raping some such woman, and as suitable women were not readily available the first one caught would be raped

54 KIKUYU SOCIAL AND POLITICAL INSTITUTIONS

by every one of them and by any other bands who might be attracted by her screams. It seems, however, that in practice the ceremonial rape was ritually reduced, at least for most of the band, to a masturbatory ejaculation on the woman's body or in her presence. Immediately after performing the act, each youth threw away the wooden ear-lobe plug and the *michee* (bundles of sticks) which indicate the status of neophyte.

Every male initiate of the Kikuyu guild was expected to *ihaka muunyu*, unless he was physically incapable of doing so, 'to prove his manhood'. It was said that until he had done so he could never have lawful intercourse with a Kikuyu woman, and consequently could not marry. The real explanation is doubtless to be found in this. The neophyte was ceremonially impure, subject to the dangerous contagion of the initiation rites. The only remedy was to pass the contagion, and so relieve himself of it, to a woman by intercourse with her. That woman must not be his future wife or the wife of any of his set mates.

The name given to the corresponding rite for girls expressed the real function much more clearly. It is *kuhuuruo mbiro ya ruenji* ('to be wiped clean from the soot of the knife'). Every female neophyte should have full intercourse with a man before she became established as a marriageable girl. Since she could not rape a man, she had to attain her end by wiles. For this reason, the rite might not be carried out for some months after she had become a *mumo*, since no man would willingly subject himself to the 'contagion of the knife'. She would have to pretend to fall a victim to the advances of a man, who must be a respectable person and not a professional taint-remover of the *mutheria wa muchii* ('cleaner of the homestead') or *mwendia ruhui* ('seller of the sword') type. None

RITUALS OF THE AGE ORGANIZATION 55

the less, as the intercourse (ritual, so far as she was concerned, though a natural consequence of a naughty girl's
desire, so far as he was supposed to be aware) had to be
complete, her time was limited, for normally she might
expect her first menses not long after initiation (though
there were medicines calculated to delay the onset) and
she would run the risk of pregnancy if she put off the act
too long. But though the rite, as described, required full
intercourse and the rupture of the hymen, it appears that
physical virginity was expected of a bride, so that here
again there was probably a ritual reduction of some sort.
Some of the elders say that girls got rid of their 'initiation
dirt' by intercourse with immature and uninitiated boys (a
heinous offence on the part of an initiated girl except for
this one purpose), who, not having reached the stage when
sex was socially important, would not suffer from the
taint.

In northern Gaki it is said that the woman with whom
a male initiate performed the rite need not be of married
status. An initiated girl would do. Consequently, he
would often wander the countryside well away from home,
either by himself or with one or two companions, in search
of a recently initiated girl with whom to *ihaka muunyu*.
Having found one, he would 'rape' her, and if she herself
had so far failed to *huuruo mbiro ya ruenji* this would not be
difficult. There was always a risk attached to it, however,
for if she had already transferred her contagion to someone
else she might raise the alarm and leave him at the mercy
of potential enemies, and even if she welcomed the
opportunity to relieve herself of her *mbiro* she might still
get him into trouble if she thought her acquiescence in the
deed, which, though obligatory, was still a misdemeanour,
might be discovered. The logic of the situation is not very
clear. It looks as though the two contagions, the male and

56 KIKUYU SOCIAL AND POLITICAL INSTITUTIONS

the female, were deemed to neutralize each other, though this is not apparently the case with the cleansing by a *mwendia ruhiu*; possibly the latter is considered to have an inexhaustible supply of male contagion which will neutralize the contagion of his female patient, but is dangerous when applied to any woman who has no contagion of her own to counteract it. But this is the sort of speculation with which a 'savage' African would not concern himself.

It is to be noticed that a plea of *kuihaka muunyu* would not have been considered by a native court a sufficient answer to a charge of rape if the woman's guardian was inconsiderate enough to make one, which he might well be if she was not suffering from the kind of taint which required for its removal the sexual services of some outsider.

The *mumo* girls pay to their seniors fees called *mote*, consisting largely of millet gruel mixed with soda (in parts of northern Kikuyu this is called *ngutu* and is not regarded strictly as a fee) and *muhothi* (*hotha*, contribute, pay a subscription) of various vegetable foods, including nowadays cooked maize cobs. The first permits them to join in dances, and the second, which provides a feast for girls only, entitles them (usually after a similar feast, provided by the senior girls, to which the *mumo* are invited) to receive instruction in various matters, such as the complicated method of handshaking affected by *airitu*, and in the proper use of ornaments and clothing, privacy, personal cleanliness, and the rules governing the practice of the limited love-making (*ngwiko*, the so-called mutual masturbation) which will henceforth be allowed between them and their warrior friends (other than blood relations).[1]

---

[1] According to the strict rule, not necessarily observed punctiliously, no touching of the genitalia was permitted. Girls were taught that the vulva must remain completely covered, not only by the *mwengu* (pubic apron) but also by the *muthuru* (long-tailed skirt), drawn between the thighs and

RITUALS OF THE AGE ORGANIZATION   57

Similarly each male *mumo* pays the *mburi ya ihaki* (goat of the entrance fee) and certain other payments[1] to his seniors, the *aanake*, and after the necessary instruction is permitted to take part in *ngwiko* and in warriors' dances.

The customary method of proclaiming the close period (*muhingo*, prohibition) between two regiments seems to have varied from place to place. In northern Kikuyu it was proclaimed at a series of *kibata* dances. A sheep was slaughtered for the usual sacrifice, and in order to make the prohibition clearly understood a boy of approximately the appropriate age was selected at each dance and shown to the people gathered there, with the explanatory remark that until he was old enough for circumcision no male initiation could take place.

In the south somewhat differing accounts are given in different areas. In the region of the Chania River it is said that some insignificant, unmarried, landless elder who by reason of his profession or otherwise was normally outside the social pale was required to take the oath (*githathi*) so that if anybody disobeyed the prohibition

tucked in at the waist. Some elders, however, appear to think that handling the mons veneris, though not the vulva, was regularly allowed. Formerly *ngwiko* was practised in the warriors' *thingira*, but latterly, there being no such building, a special temporary hut is sometimes built by three or four friends of the same set, and used for the purpose. It is often called *githunu*, the word originally applied to the large initiation hut, accommodating as many as thirty, in which the initiates, both male and female, lived during their eight days' period of seclusion, boys occupying one side and girls the other. In Metume this initiation hut is sometimes called *gaaru* or *kigaaru* and the small *ngwiko* hut *ndomo*. This latter word is also used of the hut built specially for uninitiated boys. Nowadays *ngwiko*, which has become a more or less unregulated love-making, often takes place in the *kiriri*, the girls' room in their mother's hut, but the mother usually objects to such a practice and tries to put a stop to it in various ways, such as throwing water over the lovers when she finds them there.

[1] An account of the fees payable is given below.

E

58 KIKUYU SOCIAL AND POLITICAL INSTITUTIONS

only he or his unimportant kin would suffer. If he refused to take the oath he might be put to death. The officiating elders were the *athamaki* of the ruling generation and the one before it living in the area concerned (in this case the group of *miaki* who customarily joined together for the spectacular Kibata dance). At the end of the prohibition period (nine seasons of approximately six months each) a sheep known as *ng'ondu ya kuhorohia thenge* ('sheep to pacify the he-goat') was slaughtered and the termination of the period announced. Farther south it is generally held that the prohibition was proclaimed at a series of Kibata dances at each of which a *mwati* (maiden ewe) was slaughtered, the oath having already been taken by an elder in the presence of the elders and the local section of the recently completed regiment. The stomach contents of the ewe were sprinkled round the crowd of people at the dance to indicate that everyone enclosed within the circle was subject to the operation of the oath. The carcase of the goat on which the oath was taken (the *thenge* form of oath was customary) was hidden away carefully in such a manner that it could not be got on by wild beasts, and was used again at the end of the period for the rescindment of the prohibition. This method is reminiscent of the Meru practice in the 'unswearing' of an oath.

Very little is known by any European about the Kikuyu *ituiko* (handing-over) ceremony. Some account of it is given by Kenyatta[1] and Hobley,[2] and fuller details may be expected from Leakey's forthcoming study of the southern Kikuyu. An account in the Fort Hall Political Records for 1927 refers particularly to the beginning of the handing over by the Mwangi to the Irungu generation. The following are extracts:

---

[1] *Facing Mount Kenya*, 1938.   [2] *Bantu Beliefs and Magic*, 1922.

RITUALS OF THE AGE ORGANIZATION 59

A feature of the year was the continued development of the change of Rika or generation in Kikuyu Province. Previous to the arrival of Government the transfer of power from one generation to the other occupied longer periods, as in addition to the contributions of sheep and goats the country had to be at peace, all wrongs and injustices righted and all claims settled.

The settlement of the country was then carried out by a selected gang of young men, one elder and one moran being deputed from each section who toured the district levying contributions, executing primitive justice on murderers and thieves, and settling claims. The functions of the Irungu, the present incoming Rika, are confined to the collection of sheep and goats.

When the collection of sheep and goats is complete the formal handing over of the emblem of the reigning age takes place in all parts of the country.

On each hill, a Muangi elder will cut a tree and a woman some grass. Irungu representatives will then receive permission to build a hut or Thingira. In this hut the formal handing over takes place. The emblems are the Koodoo horn called Choro which can be used as trumpet, also a small knife or razor called "ruenji" and a needle called "Mukuha" and small samples of every kind of grain food. The razor and needle are handed over as symbols of manhood and womanhood respectively. Four of the Irungu are also instructed in all ancient secrets, and in ancient customs. If one of these four is subsequently threatened with death by disease, four old men are called in before he dies so that the secrets may be imparted to them, before death.

"Igongona" or sacrifices are made, viz. one sheep and one goat of the same colour, at this ceremony.

The emblems remain in the 'thingira' guarded by moran until the commencement of the final ceremonies. . . . The hut or Thingira in which the transfer takes place is built near the Kigumu (a parasitic wild fig-tree) which was originally planted by the outgoing Rika.

60 KIKUYU SOCIAL AND POLITICAL INSTITUTIONS

The transfer of authority is further signalized by the planting nearby of a cutting from this tree.

The new tree will then be known as the tree of the incoming Rika.

When the contributions are complete one of the sons of Muthara, the deceased hereditary "doyen" of the "Ituika" ceremony, who has been selected for the function, will name a date for the commencement of the [final] ceremonies. . . .

A large central hut called Mararo with a separate door and compartments for each of the keepers of the Thingira emblems is built in a circular pattern after the style of Masai bomas. The emblems are deposited in these compartments.

Sheep and goats are killed there. The length of stay at this "mararo" is not known. The number of emblems is counted and the company proceed to the next stage.

[Five stages, i.e. places of successive ceremonies, are then named.]

Thence the complete gathering proceed to the final place of ceremony near the Ngondo River. The exact place is a secret. It is somewhere near the village of the late Muthara.

The final ceremonies of initiation are also secret.

[Meeting places for representatives of other areas are then named].

The final ceremony for the handing over of the Rika takes place on the same day for all the Kikuyu in the Kikuyu Province.

There appears to have been some variation from area to area in the number of sheep and goats payable by members of the incoming political generation. In southern Kikuyu it is said that each member pays three, one on each of three distinct occasions. In northern Kikuyu it is said that only one payment is made. But this is a stall-fed ram or he-goat. It is called *ngoima ya gukuura bururi* ('sacrificial animal for the redemption of the territory'). According to the elders in central Kikuyu, the payment

RITUALS OF THE AGE ORGANIZATION

there is very much more and they give this as one reason why Irungu has not completely taken over yet. According to these elders, the payment is roughly graded in proportion to the seniority of the individual member of the paying generation. *The marigithathi* (first-born sons, but here it means the older members of the generation, particularly heads of families) have to pay five *ngoima* each, younger members two *ngoima* each, and the youngest (small boys, including babies at the breast) one *ngoima* each. In this last grade payment is made on their behalf either by their elder brothers or, more usually, their fathers. The individual payments are spread over a considerable period, but the men of the incoming generation in a territorial unit (in this case three or four *miaki*) pool the available *ngoima* at intervals and hand them to the outgoing generation of the same unit in groups of not less than five. One for every group of five or thereabouts is handed back to the payers. It is called *ngoima ya moko* ('sacrificial ram for the forelegs') and is said to be in substitution for the one foreleg from every *ngoima* paid to which the payers are entitled. The whole arrangement is very much like that in the preliminaries to a marriage, and indeed the elders liken the one to the other, the suggestion being that the sacrificial slaughter sanctifies the union of the incoming generation with the daughter generation of its father generation, that is, with its sister generation. The incoming generation may not eat the head (*mutue*), the *mathagiro* ('fetlocks') or the entrails (*nda*) or any *moko* beast returned to them and these portions are handed back uncooked to the outgoing generation. The generation filial to the incoming generation may eat none of the meat of any of the *ngoima* beasts at all.

The common custom by which the payer of a beast can name the elders whom he wishes to receive the *maringa*

62 KIKUYU SOCIAL AND POLITICAL INSTITUTIONS

(special portions) of the beast applies, at least in central Kikuyu, to the *ngoima* paid as *ituika* fees, the recipients being elders of the outgoing generation. No elder may get more than one *iringa* from any one payer, and he himself must previously have paid a goat to his status equal in his *mwaki* before he can be named as a recipient on this or any other ceremonial occasion. In *ituika* payments a sheep or goat is held to have two *maringa* (the *ruua*, skin, and the *ruchuthi*, loin; with the latter go a *ruhonge*, rump, and a *riua*, layer of fat between the skin and muscle along the flank) and an ox three *maringa* (the *muguguta*, hide, the *mutue*, head, and the *ruhara*, rump). The expressions used are, of the payer, who names the recipients, *kuringithania maringa*, and of a recipient *kuringa iringa* ('to get—be named as the recipient of—a special portion').

The Embu and the Mbere join together for their *nduiko* (ceremony of handing over the reins of government); the Chuka hold theirs separately. Much of the procedure, and all its essential parts, are very strictly secret, as with the Kikuyu. The following brief account of the superficial aspects is based on observation of the handing-over in the Kimanthi (Thathi) division of the Embu and Mbere which began in 1932, and on conversation with participants.

To start with, the Irungu generation held meetings, attended by adult members from all parts of Embu and Mbere, to decide a suitable date on which to conduct the leaders of the Ndiiriri generation to the sacred grove in Mwea, and to select their own leaders for the occasion; such leaders would include both old and young men with the tribal status of adulthood.

On the day selected the Embu leaders and other elders of the Kimanthi division went to South Mbere (chief

RITUALS OF THE AGE ORGANIZATION 63

Kombo's) by a specified route which entailed visits to Kanyambora Hill and Chief Rumbia's. Having been joined by the selected Mbere leaders, the Ndiiriri elders were conducted by the Irungu elders to the divisional sacred grove in Mwea. This is called Bonjuki; the corresponding sacred grove of the other division is Njauri. It was necessary, in accordance with custom, to follow the original and ancient road to the grove, and no clearing of the path was permissible, though this could be done at other times. In the sacred grove a goat was ritually slaughtered. Then the elders returned to their homes. There they called meetings of the Kanyakamburi generation at the local sacred groves, which, however, the Kanyakamburi were not yet allowed to enter.

Shortly afterwards there was a meeting at Githigiri, not far from Chief Runyenje's home, another sacred grove of the Kimanthi division. At this meeting the new name of the Kanyakamburi generation, Mwita, was proclaimed. The Mwita had been named Kanyakamburi when the elders had returned from their visit to Bonjuki.

All the participants then went home and the heads of all the Mwita generation (including female) were ceremonially shaved. Individuals were chosen by the Mwita in the various local groups to act as leaders, messengers, and general executive of their generation. It is the duty of such leaders to arrange with the leaders of the other alternation to provide a sufficient number of themselves to direct the future ceremonial.

When the Mwita received instructions so to do from the Ndiiriri (now renamed Kimanthi) they went to another divisional sacred grove, Kaguma, in what was Chief Nyaki's. (The corresponding grove for the Nyangi division is Meru, near Kaguma.) The Mwita entered the grove with the Kimanthi and offered sacrifice. Then they

64 KIKUYU SOCIAL AND POLITICAL INSTITUTIONS

returned to their local groves, cleared the paths leading to them and sacrificed a goat in each. It was at this stage that the Mwita generation was considered to have replaced the Irungu generation, now called Ndure.

Later on the Kimanthi and the Mwita leaders went secretly to a divisional grove at Igambang'ombe near the Tharia River (in the territory disputed by the Mbere and the Chuka). The corresponding grove for the Nyangi division is also at Igambang'ombe. At Igambang'ombe a further sacrifice was made and prayers were offered for prosperity and freedom from disease. They then went home again.

Later still they were summoned once more, this time to the sacred rock, Rukanga, near Kaguma, where a bull was sacrificed and further prayers were offered. Portions of the meat were taken away and eaten in the local groves. Again they went home, but shortly afterwards there was another summons to Rukanga. This meeting appeared to be the most solemn of the whole series; another sacrifice was made, the sacrificial animal being a duiker or a dik-dik; some say that this animal is not killed outright, but securely fastened up and left to die, others that it is killed by suffocation. The corresponding animal in the other division is a monkey. It is at this ceremony that an oath is sworn; apparently each leader of the generation swears to maintain the constitution and to obey the customary canons of the tribe.

The final rite was the sacrifice of another goat in each of the local groves.

During the whole of the handing-over liaison was maintained between the two divisions, three elders being selected from each to report and hear what progress had been made from time to time. These six elders met in some convenient place, but not, of course, in a sacred grove.

RITUALS OF THE AGE ORGANIZATION 65

A broad distinction may be drawn between the type of ceremony in Igembe, Tigania, and Imenti on the one hand and Tharaka, Muthambi and most of Mwimbi on the other. In the former the new *nthuki* (set) 'drives' its predecessor out of office: in the latter it assumes office peacefully. The former method is called *ntuiko*, the latter *rukunyi*. In Northern Imenti Kiruja will not take over from Miriti until the Ntita warriors have proved their powers by usurping the military privileges now accorded to Gwantai (the Kemka warriors) who are the present front-line troops. (The actual fighting is nowadays abortive, as Government naturally steps in to keep the peace.) *Rukunyi* is practised in Tharaka, Muthambi and Mwimbi (except in Iruma, Kanyuru and Kerereni). *Ntuiko* is practised in the rest of Meru, though since the establishment of the Pax Britannica little real enmity has been apparent during the process, except in Muriga Mieru and Higher Abothuguchi.

According to the Mwimbi, *rukunyi* is the voluntary incorporation of a new grade of elders into the governing body of the country, which already includes the elders of the previous grades. According to the Imenti, *ntuiko* is a forcible usurpation of power. In practice, however, it is nothing of the sort; it is rather a bellicose insistence by the new set of elders on their right to join in the business of governing.

7

SOCIAL FUNCTIONS OF THE
AGE ORGANIZATION

CIRCUMCISION confers the right of marriage and procreation on persons of both sexes and is of more importance in regard to procreation than is marriage. The uninitiated mother is an abomination: the initiated but unmarried mother is just a naughty girl. The rules governing marriage and extra-marital sex relations formerly depended in part on the age organization. The strict rule that a man could not marry a daughter of a regimental mate was only maintained in the Tetu system. It is obviously incompatible with the extension of the period of formation much beyond thirteen years.

The system of marriage grouping and its variations are reflected in the laws that governed the principle of sexual hospitality. A man could have no sexual dealings with a girl who was a member of his own *irua*—that is, was initiated at the same time and place as himself—because they were initiatory brother and sister and had a common initiation 'father' and initiation 'mother'. Nor could he approach his *irua* 'brother's' wife. But apart from this and various prohibitions relating to generation and actual kinship he had the right of access to the wife of any other member of his set. At least in several of the methods of regiment formation this right was partially extended to cover other sets within the regiment. But it was not a straightforward extension to cover all the sets. Nowadays there appears to be some doubt as to what the original

SOCIAL FUNCTIONS OF AGE ORGANIZATION   67

custom really was. In Karura, for example, a majority of elders appear to hold the view that the right of sexual hospitality, so far as the initiatory bond was concerned, never did extend beyond the set. Others hold that it covered the double set, that is, two consecutive sets which had been 'caused to be circumcised together'. Others again hold that a man had the right of access to the wives of his own set and to those of sets senior to his own belonging to his regiment.

The views of the elders regarding marriage grouping vary accordingly, the general principle being that a man could not marry the daughter of a man to whose wife he had the right of access, because that daughter would be classified as his own and in fact there would be a chance, however remote, that she was biologically his own. Thus one group of elders in Karura hold that a man could marry any girl (provided there was no obstacle of generation, kinship or the like) who was not the daughter of a man of his own set. Another group hold that he could not marry the daughter of a man of his own double set, though some members of this group say that he could marry the daughter of a man of the single set other than his own provided that he had not actually exercised his right of access to her mother. A third group hold that he could not marry a daughter of a man belonging to his own set or to a set senior of his own in the same regiment.

There is a somewhat similar variety of opinion in northern Kikuyu wherever the sets were spaced more or less regularly over a considerable period. My informants in Gikondi held that a man could marry the daughter of any man other than one of his own set. In Agothi and Othaya the opinion was that a man belonging to the *muchenge* group of any regiment could marry a daughter

68 KIKUYU SOCIAL AND POLITICAL INSTITUTIONS

of a man of the *murichu* group, but not one of a man belonging to any set of the *muchenge* group which was not junior to his own. In Mathira it was held that a man could marry the daughter of a man belonging to his own regiment provided that the latter's set was junior to his own.

8

MILITARY FUNCTIONS OF THE AGE ORGANIZATION

BEFORE a recently circumcised young man could exercise political rights there was normally a period during which he must concern himself particularly with military duties. There was some degree of overlapping; well-grown boys might be expected to join with the warriors in defensive actions and even girls have been known to do so. Moreover, a young married man who had begun to take an active part in political functions might still be deemed a warrior, and in exceptional cases might still be one for a considerable time thereafter. In general, however, active military and administrative ages were distinct, apart from a necessary liaison and some direction of the former by the later.

A recently completed regiment which had 'taken over' from its predecessor acted as a police force to the ruling generation, which, together with those elders who had 'stepped down' or 'stepped up' by special payments, might be said to constitute the government. It was the *riika riene watho* ('the regiment having command') and shared in the actual administration to the extent that it could issue orders directed to the discipline of its own ranks and the social grades below it. Special parades were held from time to time (apparently normally nine during the *watho* of a regiment in Metume and Karura) and proclamations were made or orders reiterated in conjunction with the elders at Kibata dances.

70 KIKUYU SOCIAL AND POLITICAL INSTITUTIONS

In referring to the taking over by a regiment from its predecessor the stem *tuika* ('snap, break'), regularly applied to the change of ruling generation, was sometimes used, but *haruruka* ('come down, descend') was more common. It appears that in Karura special fees were payable by the incoming to the outgoing regiment, but in the north the fee was covered by the *murungano* paid by the *mumo* to the *aanake*. Thus the Mbauni set of the Mbauni regiment in Tetu paid the *murungano* goats to the *njama* (council) of the Ndumia regiment, the Mikenga set paid the Mbauni set, who passed the *chumbi* (upper jaw and head), the *githuri* (breast), the *ruchithi* (rump), *mathagiro* (lower joints of legs), and *higo* (kidneys) of each goat to Ndumia, the Nyambari set paid the Mikenga, who passed on similar portions to Ndumia and shared the rest with the Mbauni set, and the Kianuma set paid Nyambari, who similarly passed on portions to Ndumia and its predecessors in Mbauni. But in recognition of the fact that the Mbauni regiment was now complete and ready to take over Ndumia handed back a moiety of the portions to the *njama* of Mbauni.

When a regiment had taken over it had the duty of providing the main defence force and the front line troops in aggressive raids. The actual battle order in the latter was, first, the *athigani* (sing. *muthigani*), scouts, whose business was to spy out the land and bring back reports on the dispositions of the enemy, the prospect of loot, and so on. Often they brought back some evidence that stock could be raided without much trouble—a portion of the ear of a cow, for instance. The word *muthigani* acquired, particularly in the south, the meaning of spy rather than of scout and a *muthigani* was often a Dorobo or a renegade Masai who sold information to the Kikuyu and no doubt acted in a similar capacity on the other side as well. The

MILITARY FUNCTIONS OF AGE ORGANIZATION 71

advance-guard who, led by the *athigani*, would clash first with the enemy if he got there in time to protect his stock was called *ngerewani* in southern and central Kikuyu and *mbutu* in the north. It was their duty to fall back with captured cattle and prisoners and lead the enemy, if he was following, into an ambush formed by the *gitungati*, reserve. The *murima* were the rearguard; it was their duty to get away the loot as far as possible while the *gitungati* and the *ngerewani* protected their rear. In northern Gaki there was no *murima* division, but a portion of the *gitungati* fell back with captured stock. The executive portion of the *njama ya ita* (council of war; see below) stayed with the *murima* (the *gitungati* in the north) during the early stages of the raid. Its function was to receive reports, decide on movements in accordance with the tactical situation, and generally conduct the raid.

When a newly completed regiment assumed the *watho* it took charge of the sacred military objects. These were the *kinandu* and *githitu*. They correspond more or less to the *mbui ya mugongo* of the Meru (see below). The *kinandu* (the word means gourd) contained the special military *muthaiga* ('medicine') supplied by a *mundu mugo* ('medicine man') of the Agachiku or Anjiru major clan. The *githitu* ('charm'—the same word is used in Kamba for the object on which a form of oath is sworn) was also originally supplied by a *mundu mugo* of the Agachiku or Anjiru. Every large territorial unit had its sacred military objects. Mathira, for instance, had one pair, Tetu one, and so on. The objects were taken on every large-scale raid, but only one pair would normally be taken. If, say, Mathira decided on a raid and invited Tetu to help, the Mathira objects would be taken, not the Tetu. The actual keeper of the sacred objects was carefully selected. He must be a warrior with no bodily injury or blemish and his parents

72 KIKUYU SOCIAL AND POLITICAL INSTITUTIONS

must be living and must have lost no son. In an actual raid it was his duty to protect the sacred objects at all costs. He stayed with the reserve until the *ngerewani* (*mbutu*) fell back through the *gitungati*, which then became the rearguard, when he would retire with the former. He had an escort of eight or ten picked warriors. When the sacred objects were not in actual use they were kept, in the north, in the *thingira* (personal hut) of a *mundu mugo*; in the south it appears that they were kept in the keeper's mother's hut, provided that she was an aged woman no longer subject to the taints of sex. The same keeper kept the objects during the *watho* of his regiment unless he died before it ended, in which case it was handed to another selected warrior of the same *mbari*. When the sacred objects were handed over to the succeeding regiment there was a ceremony of blessing by the *mundu mugo*, who instructed the new keeper in their use.

9

POLITICAL FUNCTIONS OF THE AGE ORGANIZATION

In all the tribes there are definite post-initiation institutions having political functions to perform. Each institution is called *kiama* (pl. *biama* in the Meru group and *chiama* in Kikuyu). The functions of these bodies are not, however, by any means exclusively political. They have also social functions, and though there may be representatives of every male post-initiation set as members membership is still to some extent dependent on the individual's social status. They have, moreover, various judicial powers. This complexity of function makes it difficult to find an English word which fits them. They have been called clubs, courts, and councils. They have, however, secret rites of initiation and various grades, and perhaps the most convenient word to use is 'lodges', although in fact they may be clubs or courts or councils (legislative or otherwise) according to their functions of the moment. The native word, *kiama*, is itself too wide in meaning to suit our purpose.

Pre-Initiation Institutions

There are pre-initiation institutions similar in general set-up to the post-initiation lodges. Some of these are actually called *biama* (*chiama*) and have an entrance fee. They concern themselves with games and with playing at being grown up; probably they are largely imitations of the institutions of adults. But they are by no means negligible in function, for they inculcate a spirit of group

74 KIKUYU SOCIAL AND POLITICAL INSTITUTIONS

solidarity, mutual aid, obedience, and discipline, and provide an early opportunity for youths with an innate gift of leadership to exercise and develop it. They serve a very useful purpose in character training and prepare the young to take an efficient share in the more serious business of the community when the time arrives.

There are many such pre-initiation institutions in the Unit as a whole. The following brief descriptions of a few of them are given by way of illustration.

The institution called *kabichu* in Imenti (*kathingiriti* in Tigania and *kambaragichi* in Chuka) tests the powers of observation of the would-be entrant. Two members demonstrate their mind reading powers in front of him. One of them asks a long list of questions, such as "Where did I go yesterday? A's? B's? C's?" and so on. The other member invariably gives the right answer and the non-member is told that he can be taught thought-reading on payment of an entrance fee (a piece of chain long enough to make a ring for the right thumb of his sponsor). He may be allowed to fail the first time and then has to pay another piece of chain long enough for the little finger. The secret is then explained; the questioner stands with his big toe raised and presses it firmly to the ground to indicate the right answer when he comes to it. Only a few boys are 'taught *Kabichu*'.

In Meru proper all the large boys are expected to enter the '*kiama*' called *kiigumi* in Imenti and *uiji bu ukuru* ('youth which is mature') in Tigania. The fee is paid in tobacco to previous initiates and a quantity of food, called *njiga cha kiigumi* in Imenti, is prepared for the occasion. Two lines (each called *ruari* or *kiari*) of previous initiates, including warriors and, in Imenti, even elders, are drawn up, each man or youth being armed with a light stick. The entrants are expected to run between the lines from

POLITICAL FUNCTIONS OF AGE ORGANIZATION   75

end to end. They are naked except for a small leather apron, and may get a severe trouncing as they go through. Care is taken not to hit an entrant's face, abdomen or genitals but he may otherwise be badly knocked about.

In Imenti, Miutini, Mwimbi and Muthambi and possibly elsewhere there is a '*kiama*' called *nchibi*. Only selected boys are 'taught *nchibi*'. The fee is a piece of chain long enough to make a bracelet for the left wrist, and the neophyte is taught various aphorisms, riddles, proverbs and the like, the instruction being given in the form of songs. In addition to the fee a quantity of food (*njiga cha uringuri*) has to be supplied for the older youths (*ndinguri*). A similiar '*kiama*' in Chuka is called *gatanga*.

The Imenti '*kiama*' called *gatuuri* appears to concern itself principally with secret signs marked on sticks and paths, initiates being taught the interpretations of them. The marks used seem to be much like those on the Kikuyu riddle-picture gourd (*gichandi*).

In Kikuyu there is a boys' '*kiama*' called *ngutu*. Every *mwaki* (group of *matura* or village-groups) has (or had) its *ngutu* 'house', which is a roughly constructed hut built in a fenced or hedged courtyard to which there is a long narrow path of entrance, also fenced or hedged with planted shrubs. At each end of this path one or more poles of the *mukindu* palm (*Phoenix reclinata*) are set up, the branches being left on so that it is difficult to pass without brushing against them. Each of these poles is known as *muhiki* (bride), the implication being that touching involves payment. The entrance fee is one banana, and another banana has to be paid every time a member touches one of the 'brides'. Any inquisitive non-member who touches the palm at the more distant end is similarly fined if caught. The 'cases' are heard by the council (*njama*) of the '*kiama*'. If bananas are not coming in fast

76 KIKUYU SOCIAL AND POLITICAL INSTITUTIONS

enough the *ngutu* may go round the *mwaki* collecting subscriptions. Formerly the *ngutu* was particularly active in June and July; it has now, to a large extent, fallen into disuse.

The more obvious activities of such pre-initiation institutions are not necessarily their only concern. The *njama* of the *ngutu*, for instance, make arrangements for various games, dances and the like, and generally control the communal life of the boys of the *mwaki*.

In Chuka there is a '*kiama*' called *kagwithia* in which youths approaching circumcision are instructed by the warriors. Its members used to form the junior warriors' council both before and after circumcision, many of the fighting men being still uncircumcised.

Warriors' Institutions

In all the tribes of the Unit the warriors of each territorial area had their council (*kiama* or *njama*) which was responsible for the actual conduct of military operations, though it would consult the elders responsible for the wider issues, such as strategical plans, the timing of a campaign, alliance, and so on. Other functions were the discipline of the warriors as a whole, the instruction of junior warriors, both in tactics and in the rights and prohibitions pertaining to their sub-set, and the general policing of its area.

In the Meru group each area had its *gaaru*, a hut which served as dormitory or barracks for all its warriors. Each *gaaru* had its special name; if a warrior was asked what *buuru* he came from he would as likely as not name his *gaaru*, which defined the set of people with whom he was associated for the time being. His male *buuru*, his men friends, could include his own kin, whereas his female *buuru*, his girl friends, could not, in the limited sense in

POLITICAL FUNCTIONS OF AGE ORGANIZATION 77

which the word was used as between warriors and girls.

The council of the *gaaru* was known as *njuri ya gaaru* or as *ramare*. It was responsible, among its other duties, for the 'hardening off' of neophytes when they entered the *gaaru*. The naming of the new warrior was often used as an occasion to give him a sound thrashing. His new name had already been chosen by his father. It was in the form *muntu wa*,[1] 'man of' (frequently contracted colloquially to *nta, ntwa, nto*) followed by a word generally referring in some way to the young man's *ntagu* (namesake). This new name had been indicated to him, and the father would tell the warriors who came to fetch the neophyte to the *gaaru* what his name was to be. In the *gaaru* he was offered several names before the right one and was severely beaten at each refusal to accept the one offered.

In time of war or when raids were threatened all the warriors were expected to be in outposts which were well away from the villages. The only exceptions were the seasoned warriors detailed as an escort for the cattle (*ngitung'a ya ng'ombe*), who slept in the *gaaru* when they had brought the cattle back for the night. It was they who maintained liaison with the elders and arranged for adequate food supplies for the outposts. If a warrior who should have been in a *lai* (outpost) was found in the villages he was shamed by being driven through the densely cultivated lands (where the girls would see him) carrying a bunch of bananas on his back like a woman. Bells were attached to his thighs to attract attention, and it was made clear to the girls that they must have nothing to do with him. In Tigania, for instance, he would be called *muntu wa Mwimbi*, 'person of Mwimbi', to indicate that he was forbidden to Tigania girls.

[1] This is generally indicated by M' in the writing of the names of adult males.

78 KIKUYU SOCIAL AND POLITICAL INSTITUTIONS

The warriors' *kiama* is known as *ramare* all through the Meru group, but the Miutini and Muthambi usually call it *njuri ya gaaru* and the Igoji *njuri ya nthaka*. In general every warrior who completes his service at the *gaaru* will have entered the *ramare*. Considerable entrance fees in the form of goats and food are paid. There are secret initiation rites and the detail of the payments is also secret.

In Chuka the warriors' *kiama* is called *nchama ya gaaru* or *ya ita* or *ya riitho* ('council of the barracks' or 'of war' or 'of the patrol'). The entrance fee appears to be a goat. Paid at the same time or later, when joining the Kibogo (the first grade of the adult *kiama*), are a honey-barrel to the initiate's 'father' and two honey-barrels to the local elders.

In Embu, Mbere, and Kikuyu (including Gichugu and Ndia) the warriors' council is called *ngama ya ita* ('council of war'), but this name generally covers not only the council of the warriors themselves, but also their advisers who are no longer strictly *aanake*. Those of the council who are *aanake* form the *njama ya aanake*. In Kikuyu a distinction is sometimes made between the senior warriors' council (*njama ya aanake*) and the junior warriors' council (*njama ya aanake a mumo*). In Embu, Mbere, Gichugu, and Ndia the entrance fee to the *njama ya ita* appears to be one goat. In Kikuyu one goat (*mburi ya ihaki*) is paid soon after initiation, and two or more further goats (also called collectively *ihaki*) are paid before the initiate can call himself a *mwanake*. Payments are made to the senior grade of warriors; initiates, in fact, have to 'buy' the privileges accorded to full warriors, and the payments are not entrance fees to a *kiama* called *njama ya ita*, which, in strict usage, consists of the *athamaki* of the warrior grade and upwards responsible for the conduct of warlike operations.

POLITICAL FUNCTIONS OF AGE ORGANIZATION 79

The functions of the warriors' council were largely concerned with raiding expeditions and with defence. In the case of the Chuka this generally resolved itself into a delaying action so that the women and children and the old men would have time to get away into the forest and hide behind the line of fortifications which the warriors would try to hold.

The warriors' council was also responsible for the maintenance of discipline among the warriors and the enforcement of the traditional limits to self-indulgence in such matters as beer-drinking and relations with the other sex.

The *kirindi* of the Chuka continuously, and the *ramare* of the Meru and *njama ya aanake* of the rest when called upon, supplied the active police force for the preservation of internal order and good government. It was their business to ensure the attendance of those evil-doers on whom sentence of death had been delivered, such as habitual thieves or notorious witch-doctors, who were regarded as a menace to the tribe or a considerable territorial section of it. Such a criminal would be stretched out on a public path, pegged down with forked sticks,[1] and left to die or possibly be burned to death. The *king'ore* (crowd of people collected for this purpose) would consist largely of the warriors directed by their council. In Chuka it was the *kirindi*, instructed by the *mugongo*, who would go to tell the fathers of a pregnant uninitiated girl and her lover to bring them to the cross-roads (*gitungano*) for 'the sacrifice' (the girl and her lover were called the *nthenge*, the sacrificial or ceremonial objects). Pegged out in an imitation of the act of *coitus*, the guilty couple were left to die (frequently they were first stoned to death or beaten to death with an old type of club, called *ndivo*).

The ordinary everyday activities of the adult lodge

[1] The word used in Kikuyu is -*ambana*, peg (something) out together.

80 KIKUYU SOCIAL AND POLITICAL INSTITUTIONS

were very largely social. It was the club of the married men and its usual business was conversation about current affairs, the state of the crops, the condition of stock, recent raids and so on, with occasional stories and bits of traditional history, over a joint meal of which the menu was chiefly mutton and beer. In the Meru group the *ntani cha kiama* and in the rest the first grade, particularly the younger members, did the chores.

Elders' Institutions

The next *kiama* a man enters[1] is that of the elders, the married men. But marriage itself is not socially an important event as far as status is concerned. If one presses the point one may be told that a young married man is not strictly a *muthaka* or *mwanake*, but he continues to be regarded as such for some time to come. In Meru when an older warrior marries he may continue to sleep at the *gaaru* from time to time, and when his wife is pregnant may do so regularly, and in Kikuyu several payments, often over a considerable period, have to be made before the transition from warrior to elder is regarded as complete. From the point of view of status, the most important event in a man's life after his own circumcision is that of his first child, which marks the beginning of a new adult generation in his descent line and the consequent possibility of its extension to yet another. In principle, then, the adult *kiama* consists of men who have performed this most important function, and those seeking entrance to it are men whose first children are approaching the normal age of circumcision. In general a young man will start to pay fees soon after marriage, and

---

[1] The natives do not talk of 'entering' a *kiama*, but of 'coming out' of one or of 'being taught' *kiama* so-and-so. The former use is similar to that of the English use of 'coming out' for a girl's first introduction to society.

POLITICAL FUNCTIONS OF AGE ORGANIZATION 81

in practice the ambitious or the wealthy may enter the *kiama* at a comparatively early age. No man can have his first child circumcised until he has become a member. Childless men generally enter at the same time as members of the same set or sub-set. The adult *kiama* is therefore linked with a social status which, as has been seen, is defined in the nomenclature applied to stages of biological maturation; its functions are partly social and partly political, and though there are certain social limits set to membership its political functions make those limits anything but narrow.

In the Meru group a young married man begins soon after marriage to pay fees to the ruling set. Each set 'buys' its right to circumcise its children from the previous set in a series of *ntuto* feasts given by individuals. It is in this way that the *kiama*, which 'cuts across' the sets and may include men of every post-initiation set still living, recognizes the system of sets as an essential of the total constitution. Every locality has its special *kiama* house and every neophyte his initiatory 'father' (sponsor). The initiation rites are secret. Recently initiated members (called *ntani cha kiama* or *nthaka cha kiama*) do various menial tasks for the *kiama* as a whole. They build the house, collect firewood, slaughter stock, and divide the meat. Most of them are *miruao* of the set below the ruling set.

In the Meru group this adult *kiama* is frequently called simply *kiama*. Its distinctive name in Igembe and Tigania is *kiama otha* and in Imenti *kiama otha* or *kiama kia nkomango*. In Miutini and Igoji it is usually called *kiama kia njuguma* ('*kiama* of the knobkerry') or *kibogo*. The Muthambi use *nkomango* or *njuri ya Mwimbi*, the latter because Muthambi neophytes are 'taught *kiama*' in Mwimbi if a *kiama* house is built there first. In Tharaka the *kiama* is known as *kiama*

82 KIKUYU SOCIAL AND POLITICAL INSTITUTIONS

mwiru or *kiama kiiru* ('the black *kiama*') but *kiama otha* is also heard.

In Chuka the first grade of the adult *kiama* is called *kirindi*, in Embu *kibogo*, and in Mbere *kiama kia njonjo*. The Chuka also use *kibogo* and the Mbere *muchegara*. In Embu the payments consist of a series of goats, a quantity of beer, and two honey-barrels, and in Mbere one he-goat, one honey-barrel, honey or honey-beer, and an axe. In Chuka the payment is three goats and a maiden ewe.

In Gichugu and Ndia the first grade is called *ngariaka*. The payments consist first of nine goatskins and then of another goatskin, and there are subsequent payments of goats and millet beer. The word *ngariaka* appears to mean 'those who stay with the women' and a variant is *ngarianja*, 'those who stay at home'.

In Kikuyu proper the first grade is called *kiama kia kamatimu*. There is a great deal of variation from place to place as to the necessary preliminary payments.

In all these tribes members of the first grade of the *kiama* perform certain domestic duties for the *kiama* as a whole. They correspond more or less to the *ntani cha kiama* of the Meru group. But their standing is not quite the same in every tribe and sub-tribe. In Meru the *ntani cha kiama* are members of the *kiama*. In Chuka the *kibogo* are members and there is some degree of overlap between them and the *kirindi* in regard to menial duties. Many of the *kirindi* may still be bachelors. In Kikuyu proper it is generally held that the payment of the goat called *hako*, payable before a man takes his first bride to her new home, makes him a member of the *kiama kia kamatimu*, but does not make him a member of *kiama*. It may be said that the political functions of the *kiama* are somewhat more emphasized in Meru than in the rest, who make the appropriate social status more important as a preliminary

POLITICAL FUNCTIONS OF AGE ORGANIZATION 83

to membership. For the individual, however, the issue is partly avoided by according him a social status equal to that of his contemporaries. A childless man may become a member of the *kiama* with his own set (*riika*) because although he has no child himself his fellow members have children of an initiable age and these are his classificatory sons and daughters. The only exception appears to be Mbere, where it is asserted that a childless man may not proceed beyond the grade of *muchegara*.

In the tribes and sub-tribes which recognize distinct *kiama* grades it is the second grade which is looked upon as the *kiama* proper. The Chuka call this second grade *nkome*, but they do not distinguish clearly between *kibogo* and *nkome* and both are also called *kiama mwiru*; probably the latter is a name imported from Tharaka, and it frequently serves to cover the whole adult *kiama*. The fee is five goats. In Embu the second grade is called *kigochi*, but an intermediate grade (*ndogi*) between *kibogo* and *kigochi* is sometimes mentioned; it refers to men who have started to pay the *kigochi* fees, but have not completed payment. The Mbere call the second grade *kiama kiiru*; a man may become a member after his first child has been circumcised.

In Gichugu and Ndia the second grade is called *kiama* simply, as is the case in Kikuyu proper, where, however, it is frequently called *kiama kia matathi*, in reference to the *matathi* leaves which each member may carry and which he uses to wipe sweat from his face. When a man is admitted to this grade he is presented with a staff of office (*muthigi*); and in Metume, where *matathi* are not carried till a later stage is reached, the grade is called *kiama kia muthigi*.

The Embu, the Mbere, and the Kikuyu recognize a third grade of the *kiama*. It is particularly this grade which is empowered to deal with serious cases, such as murder,

84 KIKUYU SOCIAL AND POLITICAL INSTITUTIONS

and whose jurisdiction is regarded as extending beyond the boundaries of the individual's own locality. Members from a distance, if they are *athamaki* (*achiri*, leaders) are frequently called in to assist in important or difficult civil disputes. In Embu and Mbere this grade is called *ngome* and in Gichugu and Ndia *kiama kia itwiro* ('*kiama* of the judgement'). In Kikuyu proper it is *kiama kinene* ('the big *kiama*') or *kiama kia bururi* ('*kiama* of the countryside') in contradistinction to *kiama kia itura* ('*kiama* of the village group'), sometimes applied to the *kiama kia kamatimu*, *kiama kia mwaki* (' *kiama* of the group of *matura*') which is a name applied to the everyday working *kiama* of the most convenient deme, and *kiama kia rugongo* ('*kiama* of the ridge'). But in Karura and Metume the 'third grade of *kiama*' merely implies an *ad hoc* function; its members are not necessarily of any grade of eldership above *muthuri wa mburi ithatu*.

It would probably be more consonant with native ideas to say that the Kikuyu only recognize two *kiama* grades, the *kamatimu* (*ngariaka*) being treated as a junior *kiama* on its own rather than as a grade of the *kiama* proper. This is emphasized in Gaki, where the *kiama kia mburi imwe* ('*kiama* of one goat') corresponding to the *kiama kia matathi* ('*kiama* of the leaves') of Karura, and the *kiama kia mburi igiri* ('*kiama* of two goats'), also called *kiama kia njoho* ('*kiama* of the tying'), corresponding to the *kiama kia bururi* of Karura and Metume, are the only grades of the *kiama* proper.

Fees in Kikuyu

It is possible to draw up a lengthy list of the payments necessary before the various *chiama* or stages of *chiama* can be entered. Most of them, however, cannot be regarded as entrance fees in the sense that a man pays them voluntarily in order to acquire certain privileges or powers for

POLITICAL FUNCTIONS OF AGE ORGANIZATION 85

himself. They are rather obligatory payments associated with status. A young initiate may not wish to join in dances—possibly his physique is not such as to make him a success—but this will not exempt him (or his father on his behalf) from payment of the appropriate fee. Nor are the fees put into a common fund of a body corporate or club. They are usually consumed immediately; their function is the binding force of commensality. But they are entrance fees in the sense that a man may not enter the *kiama* appropriate to his status until he has made the payments.

The fees are regularly spoken of as goats, each fee having its special name—the goat of (*mburi ya*) something or other. Generally, however, they are paid in rams, sometimes in he-goats, and occasionally in beer or bulls. The sponsor, where there is one, gets a special payment.

The following list of payments, payable at least originally in northern Karura, will illustrate the names of various fees and the traditional reasons for requiring payment.

The initiate warrior pays or helps to pay the following fees while he is still *mundu wa mumo*. Each fee is normally a ram, payable by the individual or, in certain cases, by groups of two or more individuals together.

Mburi ya ndaka ('goat of the mud'). This is paid in theory for permission to use the earth with which warriors ornament themselves. It is sometimes called *mburi ya thiriga*, 'goat of the red ochre', but some elders say that this is a separate payment.

Mburi ya uchuru ('goat of the gruel') paid for permission to eat with the warriors. This is often paid before the *mburi ya ndaka*.

Mburi ya ithako ('goat of the amusement'), paid for permission to join in warriors' amusements.

Mburi ya ruimbo ('goat of the song') paid for permission

86 KIKUYU SOCIAL AND POLITICAL INSTITUTIONS

to join in the dances of warriors and girls. Another payment for a similar purpose is called *mburi ya kunyitana moko*, 'goat for holding one another by the hands'.

Mburi ya nda ('goat of the belly') paid for permission to eat the entrails of cattle, sheep, and goats. This does not allow the initiate to eat the entrails of certain sacrificial beasts.

Mburi ya urogi wa airitu ('goat of the bewitchment of girls') paid for instruction in the art of putting spells on girls and removing them again. When an initiated girl is sufficiently grown up, as shown by well-developed breasts, she is expected to join in the sexual amusement called *ngwiko*. If she fails to join in and will not yield to ordinary persuasion, the warriors may exercise what they deem their right of *ngwiko ya thango* ('obligatory *ngwiko*'). To do this they may put a spell on her so that she becomes ill or listless or fails to menstruate. In effect, they *thetha* her— that is, cause her to become subject to a 'ceremonial uncleanness' (*thahu*). If she promises to mend her ways and her father pays them a sheep, the warriors will remove the spell.

These fees, collectively or individually, can be called *mburi ya ihaki* ('goat of the subscription'). When a young man has paid them he is deemed to be a *mwanake*. It is said that formerly one of them had to take the form of a sheep or goat or bull captured by the initiate himself in a raid. It was then known as *mburi ya ruhiu* ('goat of the sword').

As an instance of the great degree of variation in the names of payments even in small areas the foregoing list, given by elders living just south of the Chania River, may be compared with that provided by elders from another part of Karura (near the Kamiti River). These latter omitted the *uchuru, ithako, moko, nda, urogi* and *ruhiu* goats but added *mburi ya kiko* ('goat of the hairdressing'), *mburi*

POLITICAL FUNCTIONS OF AGE ORGANIZATION 87

ya kuirorera ('goat for the watching', payable for the right to watch the senior warriors' dances), *mburi ya njaga* ('goat of nudity', payable for permission to dance, naked, with girls with uncovered breasts), and *mburi ya mutue* ('goat of the head', payable for instruction in the art of carving sheeps' heads and of removing the eyes of slaughtered beasts without bursting them). They made both the *ndaka* and *thiriga* goats obligatory and called the *ruimbo* goat *mburi ya ihaki* simply.

In some parts of Karura the 'goat of the head' is regarded as an obligatory payment by the recently initiated set to the regiment senior to its own.

There is also considerable variation as between the different sections of Kikuyu in the actual number of payments made. In Metume and Gaki the minimum number is said to be three, and in the latter the first payment is called *mburi ya murangano*, the second *mburi ya ita*, and the third *mburi ya njama ya ita*. In Karura *murangano* generally refers to some small objects, such as a braclet.

Nowadays many of the younger men are unwilling to make the outlay involved in these payments.

The next stage in a man's career is marriage. At the conclusion of the period of betrothal, which may be lengthy, he pays a fee called *mburi ya hako* ('goat of the wild honey bee') and establishes a home of his own. Some time later he pays another fee called *mburi ya ndegwa* ('goat of the ox') in Karura and *mburi ya ndundu* ('goat of the secret session') in Metume and Gaki. He is now considered to belong to the *kiama kia kamatimu* (also called *muranja* in Gaki). (The name *mburi ya hako* is also applied to the goat slaughtered when a newly-fledged warrior first kills a member of an enemy tribe.)

When he has a child, or perhaps more than one, he pays a fee called *mburi ya ndong'o* to the local elders of the

88 KIKUYU SOCIAL AND POLITICAL INSTITUTIONS

ruling generation. When his first child is approaching circumcision age or, if he wishes, some time earlier, he pays a fee called *mburi ya kiama*. He is then accounted a *muthuri wa mburi imwe* ('elder of one goat'). He also gives a feast for the local people of his own circumcision set. This is called *mbato* or *njohi ya riika* ('beer of the set'); this has nothing directly to do with the *kiama*, but the *riika* will see that he gives it before he proceeds a further stage in the *kiama*. He then pays another *mburi ya kiama* and becomes a *muthuri wa mburi igiri* ('elder of two goats')[1].

Shortly before the circumcision of his first child, he pays a fee called *mburi ya mwana* ('goat of the child') and becomes a *muthuri wa mburi ithatu* ('elder of three goats'). In Metume this fee is sometimes called *mburi ya kiriia* because it is paid at the time he has to send the *kiriia*, consisting of one *ndurume* (ram) one *mwati* (maiden ewe) and two pots (nyanjam calabash) of *njohi* (sugar-cane beer) to the father of the child's mother.[2]

After the circumcision he slaughters the *ndurume ya kuinukania* ('ram of the reunion') at his homestead.

At the stage he is ceremonially presented with a staff of office (*muthigi*) and may carry the *matathi* leaves on ceremonial occasions. He is now a member of the *kiama kia matathi* (called *kiama kia muthigi* in Metume; in Gaki, at this stage, he is a *muthuri wa mburi imwe*).

Later on he may pay a further fee. In Gaki this is called *mburi ya kuohere muthigi* ('goat of the tying of the

---

[1] *Mbato* is also used of the *njohi ya muhiriga* ('beer of the clan'), the feast given at the father's homestead to his clan (*mbari*) elders and their wives prior to the circumcision of the child. It is usually held before the *njohi ya riika*.

[2] The *mburi ya kiriia* or *ngoima ya kiriia* is often the name given to the payment made to the mother's brother when her last child is circumcised, that in respect of the first child being known as *mburi ya uihwa*. The amount of both these payments varies from clan to clan.

POLITICAL FUNCTIONS OF AGE ORGANIZATION 89

staff'); he is now presented with a staff specially cut from a *mungirima* tree (*Ochna* sp. ?) in the forest by an old member and blackened by steeping in the mud of a river bank for a considerable time, and a bunch of *matathi* or *maturanguru* leaves tied together. He is then a *muthuri wa mburi igiri* and belongs to the *kiama kia njoho*. The new *muthigi* is called *muthigi mwiru* ('black rod'), the first one being *muthigi mweru* ('white rod'). The black rod is presented at a special feast. The novice's first wife attends with him and when he receives the black rod he hands it to her and she takes it to their home. This is the last stage in the *kiama* initiations in Gaki.

In Metume and Karura a fee (sometimes called *mburi ya ngangati* in the former) is similarly payable, but there appears to be no special ceremony and it is not obligatory. The man who pays and is accepted by his predecessors becomes a *muthuri wa mburi inya* ('elder of four goats'). One more fee, sometimes called *mburi ya gutinia ngoro* ('goat for the cutting of the heart') may still be paid, and the man who pays it becomes a *muthuri wa mburi ithano* ('elder of five goats'); one more payment, called *mburi ya atonyi* ('goat of the advisers') brings the list to an end. These last two are payable only by elders who are to officiate at sacrifices and circumcisions. A man who has paid the last is called *muthuri wa mburi ithathatu* ('elder of six goats'). In Karura payment of the *mburi ya gutinia ngoro* is part of the proceedings which entitle the elder, if he belongs to the ruling generation, to hold circumcisions in his own homestead. The titles 'elder of five goats' and 'elder of six goats' are honorific and have no special meaning in relation to the judiciary.

In Karura the payment which gives a man the rank of *muthuri wa mburi inya* is sometimes called *ng'otho*, and in some areas is now held to be the same as the *mburi ya aka*

G

90 KIKUYU SOCIAL AND POLITICAL INSTITUTIONS

('goat of the women'), which must be provided by some-body each year when the rainfall is poor as it is associated with the prospects of a satisfactory harvest. Every woman of the *mwaki* wears a wristlet (*rukwaro*, pl. *ngwaro*) cut from the skin of the *mburi ya aka* on her left wrist.

It is to be noticed that there is a good deal of variation from place to place, and apparently there is some forget-fulness as to what the original custom in regard to pay-ments really was. Some hold, for instance, that according to the strict rule only one *mburi ya kiama* is payable and that a man who has paid the *mburi ya ndongo* is a *muthuri wa mburi imwe*. Other fees and feasts, which have essentially nothing to do with the *kiama*, are sometimes named as *kiama* payments. One of these is the feast, called *mathambo*, of mutton, honey-beer (*uuki*), and dolichos beans (*njahi*), which is given in Gaki to the elders of the *itura* and visiting friends when a child is approaching circumcision age.

The Higher Grades in Meru

Corresponding to some extent to the higher grades of the Kikuyu *kiama* is the *njuri* of Meru. This is known as the *njuri ya kiama* in Imenti, Miutini and Igoji, and as the *njuri ncheke* in Tigania and Igembe. Possibly the best translation of *njuri* is 'committee'; *njuri ncheke* means the 'thin (thinned out, selected) committee'. The corre-spondence between the *njuri* and the higher grades of the Kikuyu *kiama* is not complete. The thinning out in Meru is (or was) much more deliberate; it did not happen merely in the course of time; there was originally, it is said, a definite selection with the object of reducing the working *kiama* of a wide area to a committee of the most intelligent and most influential. Age status was of com-paratively slight importance; in Imenti a man could be a member while he was still a *muthaka*. There is now a

POLITICAL FUNCTIONS OF AGE ORGANIZATION 91

tendency, particularly in Igembe, for the majority of men, except the very poor, to become members sooner or later, and functional selection in the formation of 'committees' is dependent on the system of *agambi*. This brings the Meru very much into line with the Kikuyu so far as actual practice is concerned.

The *njuri* has its special house, its special secret teaching, and a secret form of oath. Each administrative area has its house, built by, or under the supervision of, the *ntani cha njuri*—that is, initiates below the ruling set.

There appears to be very little in the way of tradition regarding the origin or evolution of the *njuri*. The *kiama* itself is mentioned in the Meru myth as follows:

> When all the wrestlers were circumcised there was nothing to distinguish between them. So the oldest set thought of another way to show their seniority, and they held themselves aloof from the rest. When the others asked them why, they said, "We cannot live with you because we have come out of *kiama* and you haven't." The others said, 'We want to come out too.' The seniors said, "You cannot come out until you have been taught and have sworn an oath to forget your childhood's ways and have agreed that you may no longer do as you please but must do as the *kiama* of the grown up men directs." To this day the *kiama* settles quarrels and disputes in a peaceful manner and will not let a man be guided by his own desires alone.

According to one story, the original founder of the *njuri* was a man of the Michubu ya Ikaria *nthuki*. He lived about 1750 and his name was Kaura wa Bechau. There are several tales of his prowess and intelligence: how he managed stealthily to surround and destroy an Mbere fighting force with a band of Meru demonstrating a warriors' dance to their captors, how he won a long-distance bow-and-arrow contest by using his foot instead

92 KIKUYU SOCIAL AND POLITICAL INSTITUTIONS

of his hand to pull the bowstring back, and how he acquired many cattle by inviting the elders to a meagre beer drink and arranging with his wife to kick a dog until it yelped, and then to run into the circle with the remark, "What are we going to feed our child on now? That bitch refuses to let me milk her!" so that the elders were moved to pity. It was he, so the story says, who first thought of off-loading the dead weight of passive *kiama* members, and inaugurated an active committee from the rest by a secret initiation into an inner lodge which could enforce its will by potent curses.

Occasionally a select committee of the *njuri* of a particular area is formed. It is then called *njuri mpere*. There is no special teaching and no entrance fee. If the *agambi* of the *njuri* separate themselves from the rest and form a lodge of their own it is known as *njuri mpingire*; there is said to be a fee, but no special teaching. Such formations may illustrate the manner in which *kiama* grades arise.

Very aged men, so old that they are "sexually as pure as little children" have certain special functions. In Chuka, for instance, they are called *akuru ba ngai* ('old men of God') and officiate, often accompanied by little children, in tribal sacrifices. Such men, if they have passed through the usual *kiama* grades, are considered by some of the tribes or sub-tribes to belong to a special *kiama*, called *kiama kia mbiti* ('council of the hyenas'), although there is no special teaching and no fee. These tribes and sub-tribes are the Tharaka, the Chuka, the Muthambi, and possibly others. The *kiama kia mbiti* are called in to close cases of compensation for murder and are believed to be able to handle corpses with impunity; no doubt the name is derived from this fact, it being the practice of hyenas to dispose of the dead; in Chuka

	IMENTI	TIGANIA	MWIMBI	THARAKA	CHUKA	EMBU	MBERE	NDIA	GAKI	METUME	KARURA	
				——Kagwithia——								Transition from youth to manhood
Warriors' Council	Ramare	Ramare	Ramare	Ramare	Ita	Ita	Ita	Ita	Ita	Ita	Ita	
				——Kirindi——								Transition from warrior to family head
Adult Lodge First Grade	Nkomango	Otha	Njuguma	Mwiru	(Kibogo)	Kibogo	Njonjo	Ngariaka	Muranja	Kamatimu	Kamatimu	
Second Grade	Nkomango	Otha	Njuguma	Mwiru	(Kibogo)	Kigochi	Kiru	Kiama	Mburi Imwe	Muthigi	Matathi	First child approaching initiation
Third Grade	Nkomango	Otha	Njuguma	Mwiru	Nkome	Ngome	Ngome	Itwiro	Njoho	(Bururi)	(Kinene)	First child initiated
Senior Lodge	Njuri ya Kiama	Njuri Ncheke	Nkome									
Special Grade				Mbiti	Mbiti							Life cycle completed

SOCIAL AND POLITICAL LODGES

94 KIKUYU SOCIAL AND POLITICAL INSTITUTIONS

vultures and other carnivorous birds are sometimes called *akuru ba ngai.*

The *nkome* of Mwimbi and the *ngome* of Embu and Mbere are also credited with the power to handle corpses without incurring the death taint (*rukuu*). The former, however, is nowadays more or less identified with the *njuri ya kiama* of Imenti, and in Embu and Mbere it is only the very aged members of the *ngome* who have no further intercourse with women and are consequently considered fit and proper persons to touch dead bodies, the general principle being that a person who is incapable of passing on the taint to the other sex is incapable of getting it.

Correspondences between the Different Systems

The figure compares the lodges of the tribes and sub-tribes of the Unit. An exact comparison is not strictly possible because there is considerable variation in function between the grades in different tribes. One grade in one tribe may be the equivalent of a certain grade in another in respect of one function and of a different grade in respect of another function. The senior lodge in the Meru group, for instance, corresponds fairly closely to the third grade of the adult lodge in Kikuyu, but socially the correspondence is comparatively slight. The Ramare of the Meru group does not correspond exactly to the Njama ya Ita of the Kikuyu; the former is essentially a lodge, the latter a war council. The Kirindi of the Chuka is the active working part of the *kiama* so far as the preservation of law and order is concerned; in this respect it corresponds to the junior members of the senior lodge in Meru, who, however, can be reinforced by the Ramare, whom the Chuka (and others) sometimes call the Njuri ya Kiama; they are the executive police force of what the Chuka call *mugongo* ('ridge'), by which they mean

POLITICAL FUNCTIONS OF AGE ORGANIZATION 95

the largest territorial unit recognizing a single authority.

As we have seen, there are various alternative names for some of the lodges and grades. In some cases these alternatives appear to be borrowed and the borrowing tribe or sub-tribe occasionally applies the borrowed name to two or more grades. We are probably safe in assigning a tribal origin to the borrowed names as follows:

Ramare	Meru
Otha	Meru
Kibogo	Embu
Nkome, ngome	Chuka
Kiama kiiru, mwiru	Tharaka
Kiama kia Mbiti	Tharaka

Women's Institutions

Whether there are formally constituted women's lodges it is impossible at present to say with any certainty. Men sometimes talk of a *kiama kia aka* ('women's lodge'), but generally mean an *ndundu ya atumia* ('secret meeting of dames') in reference to some particular subject.[1]

In the Kikuyu *nwaki* a sheep is slaughtered every rainy season if the fall of rain seems likely to be inadequate to ensure the season's crops. If it is not readily forthcoming the older women in a body demand it from some head of a homestead who had not yet paid. Though they do not eat the meat, it is their business to see that the sacrifice is made. The sheep is called *mburi ya aka* ('goat of the women') or *mburi ya ng'otho*. A similar sacrifice is made when a particularly good harvest seems likely.

In Meru a girl approaching the age of circumcision

[1] For valuable accounts of women's institutions and initiation among the Meru see notes by Miss E. Mary Holding in *Man*, June 1942, and *The International Review of Missions*, July 1942.

96 KIKUYU SOCIAL AND POLITICAL INSTITUTIONS

and already betrothed has her abdomen cicatrized as an indication that she is no longer available for love affairs with any warriors other than her future husband. This is a part of her initiation, and is said to be associated with instructions in regard to marital duties. This teaching is reiterated when she eats the initiation food (*kiakira* or *gakira*), the first food taken (apart from a drink of fresh milk) after the rite of clitoridectomy. The *kiakira*, which is carried in a new half-gourd, is said to contain various common foods and medicinal herbs. It is bitter to the taste and this is explained as being due to its mixture with the urine of very old women, which will bring a *mugiro* (automatic disability) on herself or on her future children if she disobeys the teaching. As far as an illicit lover is concerned, however, it is believed to be the girl's abdominal scars (*mpano*) which will cause him to suffer from some illness of the chest. (The Imenti say the "adulterous Tigania suffer little from pulmonary tuberculosis because Tigania girls are not cicatrized".) When a man starts to cough he is advised to name the woman. If he does so it is the business of an *nkireba* of old women to deal with her. If they find her guilty a sheep is slaughtered and a small portion of its fat is set aside as a cure for the man concerned and taken to him, after certain treatment,[1] by the woman and the *nkireba*.

Men say they do not know for certain whether such gatherings of women are merely called for specific purposes or whether they are *ad hoc* committees of permanent and organized *chiama*. In the Meru group, however, the men say they think there are three institutions of girls and women with functions very much like those of the men's *kiama*, though they deal only with domestic affairs and the

[1] The woman is required to touch her breasts and rub her vulva with it. Skin scrapings from her feet are sprinkled on it.

POLITICAL FUNCTIONS OF AGE ORGANIZATION 97

affairs of women and children. The unmarried girls have *agambi*, but there may be no formal *kiama*; these *agambi* do not advertise themselves as such because they would find no men to marry them if they did. The organization into sets in Meru proper, and the use of a single name for each set all through a sub-tribe or even wider group certainly suggests that the uninitiated girls there are organized and have their *agambi*, whose functions are much like those of prefects; it is their business to maintain decorum in the set's relations with the warriors and to bring pressure to bear on girls who do not conform to the traditional standards of propriety. The young married women, the elder think, have also their *agambi*, who are sometimes called *nkatha*. This word, *nkatha*, means a good housewife in Kikuyu and in Meru is sometimes used in such expressions as *nkatha cha Nkou*, denoting a meeting of the women of Nkou for some express purpose such as attendance at initiatory rites. *Nkatha* to the Meru would seem to convey the fundamental meaning of a leading personality among the women. The *nkatha* of a *mwiriga* or *nthuki* might then be its leaders or its representatives among the women. The *nkatha* at a later stage, when their husbands are in the ruling set or upwards, are sometimes called *nkirote*. The expression *nkirote muka* merely means a clever woman or a skilled housewife. It is quite likely that the two words, *nkatha* or *nkirote*, have acquired more or less technical meanings in special contexts, as has the word *mugambi*, and that the men apply them to the women whom they suppose to be the female counterparts of their own *agambi*. Whether the women use these words to denote their leaders the men do not profess to know. There is alleged to be a body called *kagiri*[1] *ka ntichio* ('committee of

[1] Literally 'small enclosure, small circle', cf. *magiri*, fence round homestead.

98 KIKUYU SOCIAL AND POLITICAL INSTITUTIONS

crones'), which is described as a "real *kiama*". Its members are very aged women. It has the power to inflict fines on women for various faults, though what those faults may be the men, who usually have to pay the fines, do not seem to know. The fines are paid in raw vegetable products or in gruel. It is thought that the lower grades of the women's leaders have the power similarly to order certain payments. A gourd or cooking pot is commonly required, and in certain places fines in *marua* (millet beer) are not unknown. If a man offends a woman in any way he may have to pay a fine. Pressure is brought to bear on him through his wives, who may be forbidden to shave his head or cook for him until he mends his ways and pays a fine. Who exactly it is who forbids them, whether a women's *kiama* or their leaders or the local women generally, is not known.

Women have their special forms of oath, which may be sworn by a woman against herself (self-commination) in evidence that she is telling the truth or that some claim of hers is just, or as a contingent curse (commination of herself or another or others) to prevent a certain course of action or to ensure secrecy or, apparently, simply as a curse against a gross offender. A common form of women's oath in Kikuyu is *kuringa thenge ya itumbi* ('to beat the he-goat of the egg') or *ya nyungu* ('of the earthen cooking pot'), in which the egg or cooking pot is smashed.[1] In Meru the act of jumping over an aged woman's body-belt (*kamuraiking'a*[2] *ka ntindiri*) is believed to be an oath used particularly as a contingent curse. There are also special forms of oath for special purposes. One of these already

[1] *Thenge* (*nthenge*) is commonly used throughout the unit for the ritual object on which an oath is sworn.

[2] Or *kamuraitung'a*. Both forms appear to be derived from Masai (*'Ngamula' e tung'a'* and *'ngamula' e iking'a*, 'Blessing—spitting—of the people').

POLITICAL FUNCTIONS OF AGE ORGANIZATION 99

mentioned is associated with the eating of the *kiakira*, and it is probable that this was also used in the cult of *ukiama* to frighten girls who had been circumcised a second time into keeping silent on the subject. It is said that in the Meru group when a girl becomes a woman, that is, when her first child is born, a contingent curse is sworn on the amniotic fluid to regulate her future conduct as a woman and to preserve the secrets of the woman's social life; this oath was also used to hide the fact of second circumcisions practised on initiated girls at the time of childbirth. A form of curse employed by women and known throughout the Unit is the deliberate exhibition of the private parts towards the thing or person cursed. To do this is *guturama* in Kikuyu and *guturamira ng'ania* is to curse So-and-So in this way. Quarrelling women sometimes use it, and when co-wives dispute about a garden one of them, if she gets thoroughly angry, may put it out of use entirely by uncovering her person and making sexual gestures at the garden in the presence of her rival. It is to be noticed, however, that this is not a recognised and regular form of contingent curse, and Africans, except when they are inflamed by anger, find its use disgusting. But occasions when it has been solemnly employed, even by all the women of a large community, are sometimes mentioned, as when the women of a ridge have gathered together to show their disapproval of another ridge or of some overbearing personality who has annoyed them. The method is then to remove their undergarments, stand in a line with their backs towards the offender, bend forward, and lift their skirts in unison. In this manner they indicate that they will have no further social dealings with the people of the area concerned or that they do not recognise the authority of the man whom they have thus deliberately insulted.

100   KIKUYU SOCIAL AND POLITICAL INSTITUTIONS

Whether or not the women have lodges they certainly have the means and will to mobilize themselves with speed over a wide area for concerted action when they feel that their rights have been disregarded or their sphere invaded. Recent instances are not lacking. In 1934 thousands of Abothuguchi women marched on the Meru administrative station and demanded the exhumation of corpses which had been buried in accordance with an order under the Native Authority Ordinance backed by a statute of the indigenous legislative body, the reason being that the burial had caused a failure of the rains. In 1938 a number of Ndia women went to Nairobi in a body to object to the planting of grass wash-stops. In 1939 Igembe women in concerted action looted an Indian shop whose owner was not, they thought, giving them a fair price for the produce of their fields. In the same year the women of a *mwiriga* in Tigania demanded a sacrificial sheep from an aged man whose son had killed a man of a *mwiriga* with whom his own had *gichiaro* and so had caused their fields to become unfruitful.

It would seem that hitherto the women's assemblies, however constituted, have restricted their activities to matters generally regarded by the men to be within the women's sphere. These are (*a*) purely domestic affairs, (*b*) agricultural matters, such as food crops, rainfall, and the user (not the ownership) of land, and (*c*) the discipline, and the regulation of the social life, of girls and women.

Leadership

The word used for a leader in the Meru group is *mugambi* (in dialect *mwambi*) (pl. *agambi*), in Chuka *mugambi* or *muchiri* (pl. *achiri*), in Embu and Mbere *muchiri* or *muthamaki* (pl. *athamaki*) and in Kikuyu *muthamaki* (or sometimes *mumuthaki* in Gaki). *Mugambi* is derived

POLITICAL FUNCTIONS OF AGE ORGANIZATION 101

from the widespread stem *gamba* (*amba*), 'make a sound, utter, speak', and its original sense is 'spokesman'. *Muchiri* means 'judge' (*-chira*, argue the rights and wrongs of something), and *muthamaki* means 'adviser, ruler' (*-thamaka*, lead intellectually). *Muchiri* is also used in Kikuyu, generally in the more specialized sense of 'judge, one of a bench of justices'.

The Meru say "a *mugambi* is born a *mugambi*" and the Kikuyu "a *muthamaki* appoints himself in childhood". Both expressions convey the essential idea that leadership is inherent, and does not depend on the payment of an entrance fee. None the less, a leader "comes out quickly", that is to say, he proceeds to the senior grade or lodge more rapidly than most of his fellows. Leadership is a matter of personality and ability, but as certain functions, particularly the judicial and legislative, are restricted to certain grades, the natural leader is hurried along the road to seniority. In this way the system affords scope for the younger man and avoids a die-hard rule by the decrepit or the senile.

The Kikuyu say a true *muthamaki* is ruled by his head and not by his heart, he looks before he leaps, and he never loses his temper. In Meru, to quote an appendix to the 1939 Annual Report—

> . . . the—to us—somewhat indefinite quality of "ugambi" . . . is a complex of intelligence, personality, good reputation, social and economic success, and a sound heredity. Real wealth counts but is not an essential. "Ugambi" is more than a mere appointment. It implies something of the "common decency" of the English "gentleman", something of the "ungwana" of the Swahili. . . . A mugambi is *primus inter pares* because of his exceptional courage and upright character, manifested in youth and maintained in manhood. . . .

102 KIKUYU SOCIAL AND POLITICAL INSTITUTIONS

Certain clans or sub-clans are associated in the minds of others with qualities which are regarded as hereditary and likely to appear in every generation. The men of such and such a clan are abnormally hot-tempered, the women of another tend to quarrel with their co-wives, and so on. The ordinary Meru father may advise his son to avoid marriage with a girl whose family during the last few generations has produced a mental defective or a murderer, a habitual thief or a wizard, a smith or a *mwenji* ('ceremonial cleaner', like a *mwendia ruhiu*) or the child of a *mwenji* (that is, a child conceived by its mother in the process of being 'cleaned'). A *mugambi* may advise his son to marry a girl of the So-and-So "because its women bear brave warriors and fine *agambi*". Other things being equal, the son of a *mugambi* or of a wealthy man stands rather more chance of becoming a *mugambi* than does the son of a nobody, but if he lacks intelligence, personality, or drive his father's position will avail him nothing so far as leadership is concerned.

A boy's aptitude for leadership may begin to show itself in early childhood. He will lord it over the other children of the *muchii* (homestead), arrange and rule their play and lead them into mischief. He will affect a superior knowledge of the mysteries of grown-up life and be something of a hero to his social equals in the homestead.

A little later on he meets his natural rivals, the leaders of the infants of the other *michii* of his *itura*. There will be a clash of personalities and gradually one of the leaders will assume the leadership of the children of the whole *itura*.

The next stage (in Kikuyu) will be another clash of personalities between the leaders of the various *matura* in the *mwaki*. Leadership will now become more formal because the *mwaki* games are organized affairs. The dance

POLITICAL FUNCTIONS OF AGE ORGANIZATION 103

nguchu (*ngwitha* in Metume) is one in which the boys and girls of the *mwaki* join, and the strongest personality among the boys will be its natural director. The other *itura* leaders are still recognized as such, but they take a second place in the *nguchu* and other *mwaki* matters. The leader of the *nguchu* disciplines the rest and deals with any child who misbehaves himself. He is not normally the song-leader; it is personality, not voice, that counts. The choice is automatic; the natural leader takes his rightful place, though, of course, at this stage age, other things being equal, is an important factor.

When he joins the boys' '*kiama*' called *ngutu*, he will become, when old enough, the leader of it. He is then called *muchiriri* and is the president of the *ngutu* bench of justices (*njama*).

(In Gaki there is a more or less formal recognition of a young boy's leadership among his peers. Outstanding boys are called *njama*. The mother of a newly recognized *njama*, assisted by her neighbours, prepares a feast of vegetable dishes. This is divided into four. One part is used to feast the women and small girls, another the previous *njama*, another the Njoya and the fourth the Kabichu of the *mwaki*.)

Later on, if he maintains his personality and drive, he will be recognized as the leader of the youths approaching circumcision. Formerly such youths hunted various animals and used the trophies in a dance (*muhiiro, kibuiya, kirimutho*) prior to circumcision. Headdresses of colobus monkey skins were worn and capes of the skins of cerval (*kiruumi*). Buffalo were hunted "to see whether the boys were old enough for circumcision" and the horns were used in the dance, which was held when the millet harvest was in. The hunting and the dance afforded the young leader another chance to demonstrate his leadership.

104 KIKUYU SOCIAL AND POLITICAL INSTITUTIONS

After circumcision he will be the leader of the *mumo* of his *mwaki* and may then be called *muthamaki wa riika* ('leader of the age set'). He can hurry himself along by paying a special fee called *mburi ya kuambatira* ('goat for climbing'). When his *mumo* become *aanake* he will be recognized as a section leader under the command of the corresponding leader of the earliest set still on the active list of warriors. Orders to his *riika* will be passed through him. At this stage he will come in contact with other section leaders, some his seniors, others his equals, and others again his juniors. All these will be in some sense his rivals in the race for reputation, and if he is successful as a warrior (not necessarily in actual combat, but in leadership) he will be a *muthamaki* with an influence not only in his *mwaki* but in neighbouring *miaki* also.

He will remain the *muthamaki* of his *riika* in his *mwaki* and when he has paid the *hako* and the *ndong'o* he will, if he has retained his reputation for intelligence and a quiet mind, be invited to sit near the elders of the *kiama* in their determination of suits. In small cases he may be called upon for his views on the appropriate decision. This is in the nature of an intelligence test. If he succeeds he will be regarded as a *muthamaki wa chira* ('leader in law') in training and will be hurried along the road to seniority ahead of his fellows.

As his reputation for skill in the determination of suits and for knowledge of precedents grows he will become known over a wider and wider area both as a discerning judge and as an expert advocate, and when he has attained *muthigi* rank will be constantly called upon to help in difficult or important cases even at a distance.

He will still remain the *muthamaki* of his *itura* and his *mwaki* in the sense that he will be their spokesman and their representative in discussions, quarrels, and the like

POLITICAL FUNCTIONS OF AGE ORGANIZATION 105

with other *matura* and *miaki*, and if his reputation is sufficiently great in comparison with those of other available *athamaki* he will act as mouthpiece and as advocate for his *rugongo* ('ridge') or any other larger unit requiring representation in the situation of the moment.

There may thus be said to be an infinity of grades of *uthamaki*, which is essentially a quality, not a rank. It does not necessarily denote outstanding ability in the law alone or even in the law at all. It denotes the quality of leadership, and the particular type of leadership attained by any able man depends on his natural bent and on the circumstances. A *muthamaki wa ita* ('leader in war') may never develop an *uthamaki* of any other sort, but he may retain his *uthamaki* long after his warrior days are done; his genius may be military. A *muthamaki wa chira* is an outstanding personality in judicial matters, but he always takes a share in matters of administration. A *muthamaki wa bururi* ('leader of the country') is generally a politician; he is a natural leader of the people and may make use of war and legislation as his instruments of government. He is liable to develop into a local dictator if his personality is strong enough, and it is because the early European travellers came in contact with such men that they translated *muthamaki* by 'chief'. Wang'ombe of Gaki, Muru wa Mwati of Metume, and Weiyaki of Karura were *athamaki* of this sort. An *uthamaki wa bururi* could even make its influence felt outside the tribe; the Kikuyu still talk of Mwatu wa Ngoma as a famous *muthamaki wa bururi* of the Kamba. Such *athamaki*, however, were not chiefs in the sense in which the word is used by Government to-day—that is, specially appointed officers with defined powers—nor were they paramounts in the South African sense. They were the prominent personalities in a democratic system, and there was nothing hereditary

H

106 KIKUYU SOCIAL AND POLITICAL INSTITUTIONS

about *uthamaki* except in so far as the son of a natural leader might inherit something of his father's natural leadership and, being conditioned to a sense of greatness, start off with some advantage in the race for greatness.

Various insignia are sometimes worn by certain *agambi* of Meru. They do not indicate rank, but rather a recognition by their peers that the wearers have exceptional qualities or have performed outstanding deeds for the public good. Among such insignia are the following:

Ruturo rua ugambi, a specially prepared stick.

Nkome, a peculiarly fashioned double iron ring worn on the right thumb. Such a ring is said to take forty days to make. It is ceremonially blessed and presented to an outstanding *mugambi* by the Njuri.

Ntuuri ya ugambi, a belt made of chains and strips of cow-hide and ornamented with beads. Formerly the chains were obtained from the Kamba in exchange for ivory. Such a belt is presented to a *mugambi* selected by the Njuri.

Rugambi rua ugambi, a broad iron bracelet worn on the right arm and similarly presented.

Ngutuki (or *Thara*) *ya ugambi*, a monkey-skin cape, similarly presented.

Mungi jua mwariki, a special strap worn on the forehead by a *mugambi* who is recognized as a *mwariki*. The *ariki* are *agambi* who have passed through the Ramare and the Kiama kia Nkomango, are members of the Njuri ya Kiama, have completed all the sacrifices and made all the usual payments in respect of their children and have served on an Njuri Mpingire. A *mwariki* may also carry a *muthigi* (a wooden rod specially prepared and darkened by occasional soaking in mud: cf. the Kikuyu practice) and a *nyiritha ya ugambi bwa mwariki*, a fly-switch made of horse-hair or the hair of the tail of a wildebeest (*ngati*) through which sacrificial honey has been strained.

The Judicial System

Disputes within a family are settled by the father. When the father is dead the man who takes his place (his brother, or, if he is old enough, the eldest son of the senior wife) will rule, though he will generally call on close relations of the previous generation or his own for help in the settlement of disputes of a somewhat serious nature. The first-born son, for instance, will consult his paternal uncle. If co-wives become involved their fathers or their brothers may be asked to help or one or more of the women be sent temporarily to her own relations. In a dispute between paternal cousins the fathers may settle the matter amicably between themselves; the grandfather, if he is still alive, will have the final word.

No special authority, however, is passed from senior branch to senior branch indefinitely. Disputes between more distant kinsmen are not a matter for the head of the senior branch of the much extended family derived from their common ancestor exclusively. If the two families immediately concerned cannot settle a dispute, it is the business of the family heads of all the kin to do so. Authority has been distributed in much the same proportion as the common blood. In general all heads of families with a share of the blood of the nearest common ancestor of the disputants equal to that of the disputants themselves share in the authority once vested in that ancestor and may take part in the meetings to achieve a settlement of the dispute, provided that they are senior enough, that is, are members of the appropriate grade of the *kiama* (the second grade in the Embu district and Kikuyu). In practice all this means is that the members of the *kiama* belonging to a clan which is territorially intact will whenever possible settle disputes arising in the clan.

When, in Kikuyu, the two disputants are so remote in

108 KIKUYU SOCIAL AND POLITICAL INSTITUTIONS

kinship that they are not members of one clan the matter may be settled by the elders of the clans, or, if they live in one *itura* by the *kiama kia itura*, or, if they live in two *matura*, either by the elders of the two or by the *kiama kia mwaki*, which is normally the *kiama*, complete in itself, with the smallest territorial jurisdiction (limited to a group of *matura*) not based on kinship territoriality; it is the one with jurisdiction over the area in which live the people who joined in the commensal meals following the payment of the various "entrance fees" paid in the different stages in social status by the individual. (Nowadays, the population having increased considerably, the area of jurisdiction is tending to diminish and the *kiama kia itura* is taking the place of the *kiama kia mwaki*.)

A fee has to be paid to the *kiama kia mwaki* before the hearing of the matter in dispute. It is usually in the form of *njohi* (sugar-cane beer) brought by the two parties on the day of hearing, or it may be one *ngoima* (ritual ram or he-goat) paid between the two, each having contributed cash, or perhaps a goat, to make up the purchase-price. The essential idea at the back of such fees is the binding force of commensality. Those who eat or drink together thereby express their common interest and their intention to arrive at an agreement amicably; they, unlike the disputants themselves, do not divide into contending parties.

The chief concern of the *kiama kia mwaki* is the preservation of peace and equilibrium in the *mwaki*. A complainant or plaintiff usually opens the proceedings by going to his own local *muthamaki* and discussing the matter with him. He may be told there and then that the cause of action is too serious a one to be dealt with by the *mwaki*. The *muthamaki* probably knows the facts; he certainly knows that, in the majority of cases, the *mwaki* elders could, of their own knowledge of the circumstances, give the right

POLITICAL FUNCTIONS OF AGE ORGANIZATION 109

answer without difficulty, but if that answer is likely, in his opinion, to create enmity or ill-feeling between groups or individuals in the *mwaki* and so upset its peace and equilibrium he will recommend that the matter be settled by *athamaki* from outside so that the judgement, whichever way it goes, will have something of a tribal (and often supernatural) force behind it. Similarly the *kiama kia mwaki* may decide during its hearing of a case that its finding is likely to stir up strife, or that feeling is running too high and that it would be well to avoid even the appearance of taking sides, or that the argument is likely to disrupt the *kiama* itself. It may, in rare instances, come to the conclusion that it is not competent to pronounce a judgement. In all such cases it will refer the matter to an outside court.

The object of a *mwaki* judgement is to satisfy the minds of both contending parties and their kinsmen and so remove a cause of strain inside the *mwaki*. Consequently, if one party expresses himself as dissatisfied and there is any element of doubt as to the equity or peace-preserving power of the judgement he will be permitted to *chokia uhore mwakini*[1] ('return the matter to the *mwaki*'), which means that the case will be referred for judgement to a wider court.

Cases in themselves likely to cause disruption in the *mwaki*, such as homicide, or serious damage to the person, and disputes between *mbari* as to boundaries, are regularly referred at once to *athamaki* from outside.

When there is no natural community of interest between

---

[1] Used with much the same sense, though possibly wider, is *chokia uhoro riiko* ('return the matter to the fireplace')—that is, reopen a discussion over a commensal meal. *Mwakini* also means 'in the place of the fire' and the fundamental meaning of *mwaki* may refer to commensality, though the Kikuyu usually relate it to *-aka*, 'build'.

110 KIKUYU SOCIAL AND POLITICAL INSTITUTIONS

contending parties the cause of the dispute is similarly referred to a court of independent *athamaki*, if the two groups immediately concerned cannot settle the matter amicably themselves. A dispute between two people on one *mbari* naturally goes first to the kinship court, the *kiama kia mbari* (also called *kiama kia muhiriga*, particularly in Gaki), and a dispute between two persons unrelated but living in one *mwaki* naturally goes first to its court, the *kiama kia mwaki* (*kiama kia ihaki* in Metume). But when there is no such community of blood or domicile an *ad hoc* bench of independent *athamaki* is generally set up, though the *athamaki* of the kindred and the deme of each party will attend.

The Ad Hoc *Bench in Kikuyu*

When a dispute is referred to an *ad hoc* bench the rival parties have the right, up to a point, to determine the composition of that bench. Each will be permitted to choose up to the number agreed upon (two or three a side as a rule) but in practice he is always advised by his own *athamaki*. The bench, when convened, may add to its own number as it thinks fit. Some of the members, for instance, may know of a *muthamaki* somewhere else with a special knowledge of the type of case before it. The parties' *athamaki* will arrange for the convening of the bench and warn the parties to have the fees ready. Fees will amount to one or more *ngoima* each acording to the nature of the case and the value of the subject-matter.

On the appointed day the bench meets at a convenient *kiharo* (open space used for public purposes). The two parties attend with their *athamaki* and others interested in the matter. Large numbers of the general public may be present to listen to the proceedings. The parties are then heard, the plaintiff leading. Other persons alleging a

POLITICAL FUNCTIONS OF AGE ORGANIZATION 111

knowledge of the facts are also heard, the object of this stage of the trial being to give the independent *athamaki* a clear view of the issues to be determined and to ensure that persons interested and in fact the public generally are satisfied that the subject matter has been properly presented to the bench for their decision rather than a set of issues arising from some garbled or one-sided version of the facts. The essential function of this phase is the framing of the issues to be determined. Questions may be asked to clarify the issues and there is frequently a period when the matter is openly discussed by all the elders present.

Then the parties are instructed to choose *athamaki* (usually about four on each side) who together with the independent *athamaki* will constitute the court of final judgement, which sits *in camera* (*ndundu*). Close relatives of the party are not permitted because they are in effect parties to the suit. But the independent *athamaki*, if they think fit, may add one or more of the *athamaki* of the *mbari* (clan) or *mwaki* of each party to the number chosen by the parties. The *ndundu* (secret court or secret session) then retires and considers the case in private, calling any witness it thinks fit to come and give his version of the facts or clarify some point at issue.

In the meantime the animals paid as fees are being slaughtered and the meat is subsequently roasted and divided according to the grades of the various people who take part. The gall-bladders (*nyongo*) are sent to the *ndundu* and are there ritually broken as a reinforcement of the prohibition against disclosing anything which may be said by any individual in the *ndundu*, whether a member or a witness, for *uhoro wa ndundu ndumburagwo* ('the proceedings of the secret session are not broadcast').

When the *ndundu* has arrived at a decision the ceremonial meal is eaten and the judgement is pronounced in

112 KIKUYU SOCIAL AND POLITICAL INSTITUTIONS

public, usually by one of the independent *athamaki*, occasionally by a *muthamaki* of the losing side.

A dissatisfied party may be permitted to *chokia chira riiko* ('return the case to the fireplace') provided that he has not already done so. The case will then be reheard by the same court with the addition of extra independent *athamaki*. At first the *ad hoc* bench (consisting of the chosen *athamaki* of the groups and the chosen *athamaki* from outside) will merely listen to the new presentation of the case; then the new *athamaki* will, if they can, say what they think the judgement ought to be. If this differs from the judgement of the *ad hoc* bench the latter will argue the matter with the new *athamaki*, going through the subject matter issue by issue (*kihooto*, a point at issue not effectively answered by the other party). Agreement will generally be reached and judgement proclaimed accordingly; otherwise there will be a reference to the supernatural by way of oath. A party can only "return the matter" once; if it has already been returned to the *mwaki* court and consequently heard by an *ad hoc* bench it cannot be returned again.

Principles of Justice

In a consideration of the native system of justice certain general principles emerge. The first is that the rights of individuals are of minor importance in comparison with peace and equilibrium in the group or between two groups bonded in some way each with each, as by propinquity or intermarriage. The procedure adopted to achieve this purpose may have the appearance of a definite punishment, corporal or by fine, and it doubtless has some functional value of the sort. But corporal punishment is certainly intended primarily to act as a deterrent to behaviour liable to interfere with peace and equilibrium.

POLITICAL FUNCTIONS OF AGE ORGANIZATION 113

It is usually the offender's group which deals with him. A boy or youth who brings trouble on the clan by thieving may be discouraged by being beaten soundly with stinging nettles or by being soaked with water and subjected to the bites of tree-ants (Kikuyu *thambo*, Meru *mpambo*). A similar treatment may be meted out in Meru to the young husband who tends to cause a breach between two clans by ill-treatment of his wife. He may be beaten by his own clansmen with birches made of *mwiria* sticks (*Pygeum africanum*) until he promises to mend his ways; the beating is on the buttocks and may be severe enough to draw blood. Or, if he persists in unreasonable treatment of her or sends her away for no good cause his clan may tie two tree-ants' nests to his head, throw water on them and disturb the ants with twigs until they bite furiously and the offender sweats with pain. He will not be permitted to go free until he promises to slaughter a bull in expiation. Occasionally older men might be treated in the same way. An actual instance was quoted in which a man (name and sub-clan and clan given) was subjected to such treatment because he had first expelled one wife and her son and subsequently expelled another wife and her son and daughter. Very rarely married women were disciplined by whipping ordered by their own natal clans, the reason being similar—that is, a threat of disintegration of a bond through the continued misbehaviour of an individual.

The essential meaning at the back of "fines" as distinct from compensation to the injured party is the reinstatement of the offender in society, from which he has virtually expelled himself by some anti-social act. The method of the reinstatement is the eating of the animals paid as "fines", another instance of the binding force of the ritual meal. Close relations are expected to assist the offender to find the wherewithal to pay the "fine" and

114 KIKUYU SOCIAL AND POLITICAL INSTITUTIONS

compensation unless he can do so readily himself, and it is no doubt this fact which to some extent induces a sub-clan to punish the offender when his offence is frequently repeated. The habitual offender whose actions are a constant threat to the wealth and well-being of his clan or sub-clan may be summarily expelled or put to death. The same principle of clan responsibility for certain crimes and torts committed by its members still holds today in regard to fines in cash imposed by Native Tri-bunals or European courts, particularly in Meru. The size of the kinship group expected to assist depends on the amount of the fine and the wealth of the offender and his nearby kin. A fine of a few shillings he will pay himself, but if the amount is such that he will find it difficult to pay from his own immediate resources his nearest kin will help approximately in proportion to the proximity of the kinship. A full brother will pay more than a half-brother. If the fine is considerable his paternal uncles will assist, and if it is very large his paternal grandfather's brothers (or their representatives) will collect from their sons to help the offender. A man away at work in Nairobi or elsewhere will be expected to contribute a shilling or so. It is considered proper that the husbands of the offender's sisters should help, but the father and brothers of the offender's wife pay nothing. The native principle is that help can be looked for where property (such as "bride-price") has come from, not where property has gone. A family which has acquired a girl from another family is under a continuous obligation to it.

This acceptance of responsibility by the kindred of an offender has been denounced from time to time by the Administration as liable to reduce the deterrent effect of fines. But it is doubtful if there is much force in this objection. In general the wider the group which suffers as a result of an offence the stronger the public opinion against a repetition of it.

Although the principle of the maintenance of equilibrium is paramount in some respects there is a limit to its operation. The *kiama* cannot interfere with the ownership and use of property, for instance, merely to adjust an inequality of fortune between two separate kinship groups. It cannot require a kinship group with ample land to share that land in ownership or user with an overcrowded group next door.

The maintenance of peace depends upon the recognition of three principles: first, settlement by deliberation and discussion instead of seeking settlement by force; second, the correction of imbalance by compensation rather than by talion; and, third, an impersonal adjudication and assessment by the aged (in social grade) who are deemed to be beyond the partialities and impetuosities of self-interested youth.

Three stages in the mode of settlement, particularly in cases of homicide, appear to be traditionally remembered. These are settlement by force, settlement by talion, and settlement by compensation. The first of these involved the taking up of arms and generally ended in a blood feud, the second was an attempt to put an end to feuds by limiting the retributory action to the magnitude of the offence (the murder of a man was settled by the killing of the murderer or of his equal in the kinship group or, alternatively, by handing him or his brother or son over for adoption into the damaged group), and the third meant payment of the murdered man's equivalent in stock. These stages are reflected in the naming of certain of the animals slaughtered for commensal rites in compensation for a homicide. In Kikuyu ten of the goats (or one ram or bull) are called *mburi chia migwi* ('the goats of the arrows')

116   KIKUYU SOCIAL AND POLITICAL INSTITUTIONS

and the elders explain that the name implies that non-payment would mean a war of revenge. The murderer himself produces two rams called *mburi chia thiko* ('goats for the burial'), and the relatives of the murdered man provide two more, called *mburi chia thikurio* ('goats for the unburial'); these commemorate, according to the explanation given, a former right to do as one has been done by, a law of talion. Similarly, in Meru one of the slaughtered beasts is called *ntumura mata* ('loosener of the bow strings').

In cases of homicide there is occasionally practised what appears almost to be a ritual recapitulation of the three stages in the mode of settlement, seen in the manner of instituting suits for compensation. The clan of the murdered man may take up arms and invade the territory of the clan of the man believed to be the murderer. In Kikuyu the invading force is called *king'ore kia muhiriga*.[1] It goes to the banana and sugar-cane gardens of the man alleged to be the murderer or of his close patrilineal kin and proceeds to cut down the plants. When the other clan hears of this its warriors appear, also armed as though for battle. There is no actual fighting, nor in fact is there any intention to fight, for, as the Kikuyu say, *tutingihe hiti keri* ('we wouldn't give to the hyenas twice'), meaning that one death by violence no longer requires another. *Athamaki* of the senior lodge then intervene, standing between the two opposing forces and holding up their *mithigi* as a ritual reminder of their power to arbitrate. They then seat themselves on their ceremonial stools (*mirumbo*, sing. *murumbo*) and enquire what the "fighting" is about. If the alleged murderer's people agree that the accusation may be true and promise to pay the *migwi*

---

[1] Nowadays the word *king'ore* is sometimes used of any lawless band of ruffians intent on robbery or mischief.

POLITICAL FUNCTIONS OF AGE ORGANIZATION 117

goats or ram or bull called *njiga migwi* ('setter aside of arrows'), or if they fail to satisfy the *king'ore* that the murderer is not their man, the elders promise to convene an *ad hoc* bench to hear the case.

The principle of adjudication and assessment by the aged is based on the belief (formerly well justified in African society) that as a man grows older he leaves the hot-bloodedness of youth behind and is able to think and act impartially. He is less earth-bound, particularly if his immortality on earth has been, so far as he can tell, arranged for satisfactorily, that is, he has several healthy, prosperous descendants in the patrilineal line. (The curse of a childless old man is held to be especially baneful.) The word for elder (*muthuri*) is itself derived by the Kikuyu from *thura*, 'pick and choose', and denotes a man who selects carefully, one who deliberates and does not come to hasty conclusions. The general idea is neatly expressed by the Kikuyu in the saying *mburi nguru nditi-hagira tuhu* ('an old goat does not spit for nothing'; the word *tiha*, spit, referring particularly in this case to the snort and slobber of the he-goat when sexually excited). They also put it more directly and politely thus: *andu akuru matiaragia maheni* ('old people do not tell lies'). *Athamaki* who engage in litigation are supposed to be especially free from bias; impartiality in argument is in fact one of the qualities which have brought them to the fore. A *muthamaki* chosen by a plaintiff or defendant of his own kin or residence to represent him in a civil suit will often warn his client *ndingiguteithia na chira no 'guteithirie na kuruta* ('I would not help you in the case except to help you in the paying'), implying that he will not twist the argument to suit his client's case if he believes him in the wrong, but he will give him some assistance in meeting the judgement debt if the judgement goes against him.

118 KIKUYU SOCIAL AND POLITICAL INSTITUTIONS

However, it is not to be supposed that these high principles were always followed or that impetuous young men were always ready to subordinate their interests to them. It is related that from time to time the *aanake* got out of hand and settled clan disputes by actual fighting and that an *ad hoc* bench occasionally refused to proclaim its judgement until it was well away from excited bands of warriors, and would shout its finding from the comparative safety of a distant ridge.

Another principle that emerges is that the administration of justice is based on equity rather than on a codified law. The Kikuyu say *tutiri na mutugo tiga kuigwa uhoro wa mundu na mundu* ('we have no code apart from hearing the words of person and person'), by which they mean that there is no standard yardstick to be used in the meting out of justice. Such principles as burden of proof and *res judicata* cannot be invoked to override what the court conceives to be the natural justice of the case or the best adjustment of a disagreement. In civil suits *ex parte* judgements are practically unknown because in pronouncing such a judgement the court will have failed *kuigwa uhoro wa mundu na mundu* ('to hear what both sides have to say').

Nevertheless, the widely held view that Africans have not yet evolved a code of law requires some qualification. Every tribe has a code, but it is a code of general principles, not of detail. Every judgement must conform to it, though the principles are applied with a latitude unknown in European law. The rights in property vested in the kinship group, for instance, may not be invaded. But within the group equity and equilibrium may be powerful determinants in the allocation or redistribution of property.

Secondly, as regards compensation for homicide and

POLITICAL FUNCTIONS OF AGE ORGANIZATION 119

damage to the person. An actual scale of damages is laid down and is rarely disregarded. To some extent the same applies to theft. The naming and amounts of the payments in the case of homicide seem to suggest a deliberate codification at some time or other based on the magical significance of numbers. The Kikuyu of Gaki and Metume call the compensation for the killing of a male *igana na kagana* ('a hundred and a little hundred', i.e. a hundred and ten) in reference to the number of sheep or goats payable (the Karura Kikuyu call it *igana ria gakumi*— 'the hundred and the insignificant ten'). The killing of a female is compensated for by the payment of thirty goats and three rams (or, in Metume, forty goats and four rams)[1], apparently based on the stock value of a female ("bride-price") in continuity exchanges ("bride-price" in Kikuyu has increased very considerably in recent years). In Meru the normal compensation for a male is five cows or heifers, five bulls, and five maiden she-goats. But if it is decided that the death was really due to illness though possibly hastened by the blow the compensation will be *ntongoko*, not *nyamuru*, and will amount to one heifer, one bull, and one ewe lamb (the bull is eaten by the elders of both sides). In Tigania this payment is called *mirongo ithatu* ('the thirty'), presumably based on the original value in goats; this *mirongo ithatu* is the basis of payments for various other torts in Tigania and Igembe. Twice and ten times are basic rates of compensation in Kikuyu; seven times is a basic rate in Meru. In the more serious types of damages when compensation cannot readily be made in kind it is assessed in stock, one goat being taken as the unit. The amount payable in respect of a stolen beast which cannot be returned (having been lost or slaughtered

---

[1] But an African Law Panel in Fort Hall has recently declared the compensation for murder of a female to be sixty goats and six rams.

120 KIKUYU SOCIAL AND POLITICAL INSTITUTIONS

or sold outside the tribe) is ten times its value in Kikuyu and seven times in Meru; in the latter the payment is known as *nyamu* or *mugwanja* ('seven'). In Kikuyu a finger joint is valued at one goat and the compensation payable for causing the loss of a joint is ten goats. All such compensations have to be accompanied by *ngoima* (sacrificial rams or he-goats) to be ea^en by the elders, in general every group of ten goats reauiring one *ngoima*. The theft of a honey barrel or of hor..y from it is dealt with similarly. In Kikuyu the honcy thief first pays the *ngoima ya kunungura* ('the ram to remove the smell') and then ten goats in compensation. In Meru he pays *nyamu*—that is, seven goats and a bull or ram for the elders. The Tharaka say that to open another man's honey barrel is like "opening his wife", the compensation for which is (or was originally) *nyamu*.

Thirdly, there is an indigenous statutory law, consisting of edicts issued from time to time by the legislative body, and though such laws are few and far between they constitute a partial code of law proclaimed by statute.

And, fourthly, case law is a potent factor in the assessment of individual decrees. A *muthamaki* or *mugambi* depends for his judicial reputation very largely on his knowledge of the principles on which the judgements in previous cases have been based, and this, though theoretically it only strengthens or reiterates early principles of common law and custom, in practice tends to codify the detailed findings in celebrated cases into precedents which acquire the force of law.

A third principle that emerges is that the best court to adjudicate on any particular case is one that knows all about it to begin with and is in fact personally interested in it to the extent that it is its own kinship group or deme which may be disrupted if an amicable settlement is not

POLITICAL FUNCTIONS OF AGE ORGANIZATION 121

arrived at. To arrive at such a settlement a knowledge of the facts is necessary, and the best way to acquire such knowledge is to have lived where the facts were everyday affairs. A court which of its own personal experience and environment has the facts at its finger tips has a better knowledge of them than one which has to depend on a string of individually garbled versions. And a judgement arrived at by agreement between the elders of two contending parties is more likely to be satisfying in the long run (that is, equilibrium maintaining) than one arrived at by an independent court which has no immediate concern with equilibrium. This, however, does not mean that the African does not recognize the value of impartiality. His theory is rather that the *muthamaki* or *mugambi* should be impartial even though he be essentially a party to the suit (as when a close relative of his is plaintiff or defendant). Formerly the submission of a suit to an *ad hoc* independent court implied a partiality (whether justifiable or not) in the kinship group or deme which was such that no agreement could be reached. In judicial matters the African distinguishes more clearly than the European between impartiality and independence; this distinction depends on religious sanctions to a large extent, on an ingrained belief that there is an automatic supernatural readjustment when the laws of natural justice have been disregarded. This belief is stronger in the older men, though even among them it tends to vanish, but the younger men will point out how the patrilineal descendants of So-and-So, who obtained his wives and property unlawfully, have failed to flourish. But the *ad hoc* court itself, if it finds there is a definite cleavage of expressed opinion not only between the parties but between the aged and the *athamaki* of the two sides, will call in witnesses who, though likely to know the

122 KIKUYU SOCIAL AND POLITICAL INSTITUTIONS

facts, are less likely to be biassed, such as old men living near the contending groups but having no relationship with either, particularly *ahoi* ('beggars') or *athami* (immigrants). In Kikuyu such witnesses, knowing all about the cause of action, but having no personal interest in it, are distinguished from the rest by being called *agikuyu*—that is Kikuyu simply, people who could make no claims themselves and probably have no prejudice in respect of the matter in dispute.

It will be seen that the practice of the *ad hoc* independent court is strikingly similar to that of an English court of justice. But there are essential differences. The African court includes and may co-opt *athamaki* of the parties' groups, though it will rarely include or co-opt people who, in the English court, could be reasonably joined as plaintiffs or defendants. The function of the native court remains adjustment and the maintenance of equilibrium, limited only by the native principles of equity. It may not give a judgement based on some point of law alone which is unrelated to the facts. The suit must be determined on facts, not on such legal principles as limitation or burden of proof. If the facts are not sufficiently clear, the court may proceed to judgement by adjustment, as, for instance, by a division of the property in question, or it may admit defeat and refer the suit (or permit its reference) to the supernatural.

Judicial Oaths

Reference to the supernatural can be made in various ways. The simplest is the "trial by ordeal", as in the handling of a hot iron (*gikama*) in Meru. Africans do not appear to think that the efficacy of the ordeal rests on a direct reply from God or from ancestral spirits; it is just in "the nature of things", which, of course, may be

POLITICAL FUNCTIONS OF AGE ORGANIZATION 123

considered by the African (and others) to amount to much the same. Probably the *gikama* ordeal of the Meru is associated with the potency of curses uttered by a smith and the general avoidance of any intercourse with smiths by persons who are not smiths themselves, for *gikama* is the crude iron produced by smiths from *muthanga wa ikama* (iron-bearing sand).

In serious cases, such as homicide and disputed claims to land, and sometimes in less serious cases reference to the supernatural is made by some sort of oath and sacrifice. The Kikuyu recognize three main types, *Kunyua muuma* ('to drink what comes out')[1], *kuringa thenge* ('to strike the he-goat'), and *kuringa githathi* ('to strike the great red earth' or perhaps 'potent ironstone')[2]. There are several forms of the first two. These and the *githathi*, which is a specialized form of the second, have been sufficiently described elsewhere. In the rest of the Unit the *muuma* and *thenge* types are the most important. A brief description of one form of each type as practised in Mwimbi will be given here.

The first is known as *muuma wa ng'ondu* ('oath of the sheep') and is used when the *kiama* is unable to satisfy itself as to the facts in a suit for the payment of an alleged debt. Each party brings a sheep or a goat. These animals are suffocated by holding the mouth and nose and are then skinned; a small piece of skin is left on the chest.

---

[1] The Beechers, in their dictionary, give *muuma* the meaning 'that which makes the truth come out'. But it is possible the word is of Dorobo origin (cf. Suk *muma*).

[2] Kikuyu explain *thathi* as the equivalent of *thiriga*, red ochre. The late Colonel O. F. Watkins thought that some *githathi* stones were Palaeolithic implements, and Sir A. de V. Wade stated in an early note that some were meteorites (Political Record). The power of the *githathi* may possibly depend on the magical properties of ironstone. The same idea appears in some forms of *thenge* oath, the 'stone' used for battering the goat being a lump of slag (*ngangai*) produced in smelting.

124 KIKUYU SOCIAL AND POLITICAL INSTITUTIONS

Small portions of the meat from all the main sections of the carcase are then placed in a small hole in the ground or wrapped in banana leaves or skewered together on a stick. One party then declares his version of the facts, fact by fact, throwing one bit of meat over his head and eating the next bit raw with every statement and saying "May God see me!" after each. The other party acts similarly. If a hole has been used it is then filled up. The elders allow a period of one year for the oath to work in some such phrase as "when the maize is like this maize again the truth will be known". Any meat left over and not intended for the oath is eaten by the elders. The oath is deemed to have given judgement when one of the parties dies.

The other form of oath is used particularly in cases of compensation for homicide when the accused person denies complicity.[1] He is required to bring a sheep or goat. A very aged woman shaves the animal at a considerable distance from the place where the oath will be administered. She starts by shaving the forehead and then shaves small patches all over the animal's skin. Elders of the *nkome*, who are with her, then close all its bodily apertures by skewering the skin or flesh together with thorns or sharp bits of wood, usually of the *muraga* shrub (*Muraga* or *muraa, Catha edulis*). The mouth, nostrils, eyes, ears, anus, and sheath or vulva are completely closed in this way. The animal is then taken to the place where the accusing clan and the accused and his clan are gathered together. Women and girls are not present at the subsequent proceedings. The accused lifts the animal and

---

[1] Another form of Mwimbi oath used in similar circumstances requires the accused to drink water in which *nkome* elders have washed the deceased's garments, or, if the body is far advanced in decay before it is discovered, to drink water from the skull.

POLITICAL FUNCTIONS OF AGE ORGANIZATION 125

carries it on his back, with a foreleg on each side of his neck, held by its feet, round his assembled clan, declaring as he goes that he did not kill the deceased or do anything which might have caused his death or see him killed, and that he knows nothing whatsoever of the matter. He is prompted by an elder, who tells him what to say. Having walked round his clansmen, he throws the animal over his head on to the ground and then lifts it again and, led by the elders, hurls it into a large fire which has been prepared a short way off. If the animal is not already dead from suffocation, it is very quickly burnt to death. Alternatively, it can be thrown into a river and drowned. A period of one year is allowed for the action of the oath; it is considered to have proved the complicity of the accused or of one of his close patrilineal relations if one of them dies within that time, in which case compensation must be paid. If there has been no such death by the end of the period, the accused will ask the *nkome* to arrange a ceremony of purification. During the year or until compensation is paid he has not been permitted to shave or be shaved. At the purification the aged woman (or another if she is not available) shaves a patch in the front of his head and he is then permitted to shave as usual. From the time of the taking of the oath until the purification neither he nor any of his clansmen who were in the group round which he carried the animal may have sexual intercourse. This form of oath is frequently known as *nkumbuko* ('the walking round'), but the same word is used of other ceremonies of which processions round the outskirts form a part, such as those performed for the protection of a homestead or a *mwiriga* from pestilence or witchcraft.

It is to be noticed that though this form of oath corresponds in function to the *thenge* or *githathi* type of the Kikuyu oath there is not a complete correspondence

126 KIKUYU SOCIAL AND POLITICAL INSTITUTIONS

between the types used by the two tribes. An oath in Mwimbi very similar in general pattern to the *kuringa thenge* of Kikuyu and called *kuringa nthenge* by the Mwimbi is considered by the latter to be a *muuma* oath. The fact is that there is no hard and fast line of demarcation in the functions of the various types, though in general in Kikuyu it is held that the *muuma* will kill one of two disputing individuals of one clan, while the *thenge* (and particularly the *githathi* form of it) decides between two clans and may destroy the whole of the offending clan, even portions of it which may be hundreds of miles away and have no knowledge of the cause of action.

The walking round in the Mwimbi *nkumbuko* oath affords the chance to exclude certain clansmen from the operation of the oath by their exclusion from the assembled group. A similar exclusion of certain close relations is a common practice; such persons are excluded by permission of the presiding elders and are usually the aged and the sick and ailing who stand a considerable chance of dying anyway. In Meru proper there is sometimes argument as to who should be excluded.

In Imenti it is held that an oath can be "unsworn" or its terms changed by a further oath on any of the remains of the animal first sacrificed. Such remains are therefore very jealously guarded by the side which did not swear the oath, and care is even taken that the deponent does not hide a fragment of the animal's fat under his finger-nail or a morsel of its meat in his mouth, for this could enable him to amend the oath to something which would lessen or annul the risk. He is not actually searched, but his actions are carefully watched.

There is a good deal of variation between tribes as to the period which must elapse before an oath can be deemed to be inoperative. In Meru it is a year, in Kikuyu seven

POLITICAL FUNCTIONS OF AGE ORGANIZATION 127

seasons (approximately three and a half years). But it is considered that if it is going to operate at all it will generally operate quickly. The Meru method (which is normally a unilateral oath, sworn by the claimant in a civil suit, unlike the Kikuyu method, which is normally bilateral, sworn by both parties) permits an intentional cancellation of the oath and consequently a cessation of its killing power. When the swearer, having perjured himself, sees one of his kinship group fall sick or possibly hears that such a relation has died he will (advised by his *agambi*) go to the other party, admit that his claim was false, and beg him to allow a ceremonial unswearing of his original oath, the goatskin, which the defendant's kin has carefully preserved (so as to prevent a secret cancellation of the oath), being used for the purpose. The Meru say that if this was not done the original oath would eventually kill the swearer's kinship group completely, apart from those specifically excluded at the swearing. (Frequently it is those who are included in the scope of operation of the oath, not those excluded from it, who are named by the elders before the administration of the oath, the reason being apparently that otherwise more distant kindred might be killed unfairly. The oath seems to be peculiarly indiscriminate in its action. In one recorded case the man it killed was an innocent *mugambi* who had advised his kinsmen very strongly not to take it.) Obviously the Meru system forbids the settlement by oath of a dispute between two clansmen, since the oath might prove the plaintiff in the wrong by killing the defendant. It appears that this was probably originally the case in Kikuyu also, and this was perhaps one reason why the elders of a clan did their best to settle their own affairs, as the procedure of an *ad hoc* bench frequently involved some killing form of oath. Nowadays, however, recourse to the

128 KIKUYU SOCIAL AND POLITICAL INSTITUTIONS

supernatural, even to the *thenge* form of oath, sometimes occurs among close relatives, and many Kikuyu hold that the oath will kill the perjurer only, an early symptom being some irritating skin affection, though others maintain that the first sign of its operation is the death of his wife or child. This reduction of the range of the kinship group in Kikuyu in the operation of the supernatural is in accordance with a general reduction of its functional range in the social pattern of the tribe.

The prohibition against sexual activity, remarked in the Mwimbi *nkumbuko* oath, applies to serious oaths all through the Unit. The Kikuyu even say that all entire male animals belonging to the swearer's kinship group must be disposed of or castrated or shut away before the oath is taken. It may be imagined that the prohibition, when it affected a wide kinship group, would operate strongly as a deterrent to any frivolous reference to the supernatural, for apart from a natural reluctance on the part of young married people to abstain for a period which might extend to a whole planting season or more the kinship group was always wanting children. It is said that the Kikuyu *ngwiko* was not interrupted by the oath because "that was only fun, not intercourse".

Enforcement of Judgements

It appears that formerly the judgements of a properly constituted bench consisting of members of the appropriate lodge or grade were usually complied with promptly. But if a judgement debtor failed to pay and persisted in his recalcitrance he would be ostracized, excommunicated from society. He was "shut out" (*hinga*, 'close', or one of its variants, was the word used). His relatives and neighbours would show their disapproval by declining to talk or eat with him. His wife would suffer

POLITICAL FUNCTIONS OF AGE ORGANIZATION 129

similarly; she would get none of the customary help from other women, nor could she join in the usual satisfying gossip; she would be made aware of much whispering about the woman who was so mean or insignificant that she would not or could not get her husband to pay his lawful debts.

In larger matters, such as those which had been referred to arbitration by an independent bench, continued failure to comply would involve a ceremonial form of ostracism. The non-co-operator would be publicly proclaimed an outlaw. In Embu, for instance, this was done at a *kibata* dance or at a special gathering (*mbiriri*) of the local people. Sometimes, as in Nyeri, this meant that his private property was no longer safe; if his goats were stolen there was no redress. He and his family would get no outside help either in the fields or in the homestead. His wife would find nobody willing to help her with her planting, weeding, or harvesting or in drawing water or fetching fire or firewood. No one would shave her head for her. The man himself would be permitted to take no part in the social life of his peers. His sons would similarly find themselves excluded from the privileges appropriate to their status. Altogether the delinquent would be subjected to such a social pressure that he would be forced sooner or later to give way.

Actual attachment of property in execution of a judgement debt is not impossible, warriors or junior members of the lodge serving as officers of the court. In Meru, for instance, the common practice is to send two members of the *njuri ncheke* or of the *kiama otha* accompanied by *ntani cha kiama* to require a settlement. The two seniors are decorated with the usual markings of their status. They are known as *atunguri*; one must be Kiruka, one Ntiba. They go to the homestead of the man whose property is to

130 KIKUYU SOCIAL AND POLITICAL INSTITUTIONS

be attached, in company with *agambi* of his *mwiriga* (clan or village group). He will recognize them as elders lawfully executing an attachment of his property and will demonstrate this recognition by offering them a token, known as *mbanikiro ya kiama* (it is a small quantity of gruel or tobacco as a rule), which signifies agreement with the legality of the attachment, though not necessarily with the justice of it.

Essentials of the Judicial System

The foregoing description of the judicial system may be summarized as follows. Judicial powers in respect of groups wider than the family are vested in a body corporate including all those members of a formal lodge who live within the group or groups concerned. Its findings are intended to preserve a stable equilibrium by the relief of strains arising in the group or between two groups or more. It therefore attempts a form of justice by agreement, its judgements capable of periodical amendment to suit a change in situation, rather than a form of justice by immutable decree. Reference to an *ad hoc* board of arbitration is, however, possible when for any reason settlement by the group or groups is difficult or undesirable, and reference to the drastic justice of the supernatural is possible when arbitration fails. A code of legal principles is recognized but it permits a wide discretion and there is no detailed code of practice or procedure. The criminal law normally applies to habitual offenders only, and offences against the person or the property of an individual or narrow group[1] are treated

[1] It sounds ridiculous to talk of "offences against the person of a narrow group". But to the African it is not ridiculous, and in practice the compensation payable may go to the narrow group of patrilineal or matrilineal kin, the individual damaged or his next-of-kin getting no share at all.

POLITICAL FUNCTIONS OF AGE ORGANIZATION 131

publicly[1] as civil debts, the compensations payable being some multiple of the real value or of a standard *ad hoc* evaluation, the multiple varying with the type of damage. Findings are implemented as a rule by means of social, religious, or supernatural sanctions, but legal sanctions are not entirely absent.

Legislation

Legislation is a function of the senior lodge or the senior rank of the elders' lodge. The existence of a so-called "ruling age" or "ruling generation", however, complicates the situation to some extent. Theoretically the members of the senior lodge or rank who are also members of the ruling age or generation are the legislative body as long as their age or generation is in power. But in practice the lodge does not allow this splitting of itself into two functionally distinct divisions. *Athamaki* or *agambi* of the ruling generation (real or artificial) may proclaim the law but they will rarely have been solely responsible for the passing of it. This is particularly the case in Meru proper, where even the proclamation must be made jointly, that is, by *njuri* members representing both age-divisions Kiruka and Ntiba. A law passed and promulgated by the ruling grade alone would have the force of law during its rule, but not a moment longer. There would probably be a deliberate repeal of it in fact when the following grade assumed the right to govern at the next *ntuiko*. This is a symptom of the intense jealousy (*ngoga*) between the two divisions.

Curiously enough, it is in the matter of imported institutions that insistence on its "rights" by the ruling age

[1] Privately they could be treated in certain circumstances as crimes against the individual or narrow group. A thief caught *in flagrante delicto* could be killed or tortured. Theft was not treated as an offence against "the State" until it became habitual.

132 KIKUYU SOCIAL AND POLITICAL INSTITUTIONS

or generation is the strongest. In Nyeri it is held that the ruling generation is now Irungu and the elders say that if the matter had been left to them all the Government Chiefs would be Irungu; Mwangi chiefs, however capable and acceptable as chiefs, would have been deposed. In Meru proper a good deal of the "fitina" against individual chiefs and other Government employees has been due to this rivalry, and considerable trouble has been caused from time to time because this fact passed unrecognized. The following extract from the Meru Annual Report for 1941 will serve to illustrate the point.

The most troublesome effect of the ntuiko . . . occurred in Igembe and it was some time before its connection with the ntuiko was recognized. The trouble took the form of concerted fitina against Chief M'Imathiu Ithaime of Maua, and developed into a passive resistance to all his attempts to carry on the administration of his location. Several months of careful investigation were necessary before the real trouble could be elucidated, the reason being that all the people concerned had sworn a secret oath to disclose none of the real facts. When the true story came to light it was found to affect the whole of Igembe and to date back to many years ago. Very early in the history of British administration the Gwantai (Kaburia) age-grade decided to take concerted action to prevent any appointment, particularly of Chiefs, from among people of the Kiruka age-division, their own age-division being Ntiba. This, they thought, would be a very effective and, of course, new way of increasing the power of their own age-division at the expense of their rivals. If their decision had been followed in fact it would have meant that there could be no appointment from the Gichungi (Kiramana) or the Itharie (Miriti) age-grades. It seems that when appointments were actually made from Gichungi the Kiramunya endeavoured by various means to put Gwantai's decision into effect and were successful by underhand means in getting some of the Gichungi

POLITICAL FUNCTIONS OF AGE ORGANIZATION 133

appointments cancelled. But they were not successful in every case and some of the leading Kiramunya were badly treated. The appointment of Chief M'Imathiu in 1939 was contrary to Gwantai's decision and was consequently not much to the liking of Kiramunya, who were on the point of handing over to Itharie, the age-grade to which M'Imathiu belonged. At the meeting to determine to whom the appointment should be given the then District Commissioner made some enquiries as to the possibility of amalgamating the very small Maua location with one of its neighbours, this being in accordance with general policy. But two of the Chiefs of neighbouring locations belonged to Kiramunya and the most influential Mugambi, who had previously suffered at the hands of Gichungi, of the third location was of Kiramunya too. These men, knowing that M'Imathiu was a man of great personality and influence, being a leading Mugambi of Itharie, feared that (as they put it when they eventually "came clean") M'Imathiu and consequently Itharie would "swallow" the whole of Igembe, and this would be contrary to their own interests and to the decision of Gwantai to exclude the Kiruka age-division from Government appointments. They therefore got together secretly and thought out ways of stirring up feeling against M'Imathiu so that he might be deposed. It is probable that the Chiefs themselves kept aloof from any such fitina but they certainly took part in lighting the fuse which, they hoped, would eventually blow M'Imathiu and Itharie sky-high while they themselves sat back in safety. They dropped hints, in fact, to other leading Agambi of Kiramunya which suggested that the Ntiba age-division was in danger of being ousted altogether by Kiruka and that M'Imathiu was the ringleader in a concerted move to this end. The leading unofficial men of Kiramunya set to work very cleverly and stirred up feeling against M'Imathiu among the people of his own age-grade, using particularly every kind of reasonable or unreasonable disgruntlement that could be worked up into a complaint. In this they were helped by the presence in the Maua location of two pretenders to the Chiefship who based

134 KIKUYU SOCIAL AND POLITICAL INSTITUTIONS

their claims on the fact that their families had provided Chiefs or Headmen in the past. The first effect of all this underground agitation was a deputation of men, mostly young, who called themselves the Njuri Ncheke of Maua and Antubochio—which they had no right to do—and demanded the dismissal of Chief M'Imathiu on the grounds, among others, of extortion and the use of witchcraft. They could substantiate none of the charges and returned to Igembe with the knowledge that Chief M'Imathiu would retain his appointment. This failure of the first attack did not satisfy the Kiramunya in the background and they accordingly continued to pull strings and managed to start a campaign of passive resistance. The leading Agambi of the whole of Igembe were then called in and invited to settle the trouble. But when, after a sufficient period, it became known that they had taken no steps to do so it became clear that they themselves were involved and that they had probably sworn a secret oath of silence and non-co-operation. They were then called in again and were made to understand that unless they were prepared for the exclusion of the Agambi and the indigenous bodies from all part in the administration of Igembe they must get the oath "unsworn" and must then tell the true story of the origin of the trouble. They went back to Igembe feeling rather ashamed of themselves and they asked that M'Murithi, President of the Imenti Tribunal, and Interpreter M'Muraa should accompany them and be present at the "unswearing" as representatives of the District Commissioner. This was done and at the "unswearing" the true story as given above came out. It was also agreed that the charges levelled against Chief M'Imathiu were entirely without foundation and that he had done nothing that a good Chief should not do. Chief M'Imathiu's attitude throughout was entirely correct and in his share in the oath of reconciliation following the "unswearing" of the secret oath he made it clear that though he sought no aggrandisement either for himself or his age-grade if he were required by Government to assume the administration of a larger location ("even if it be from Mbirigata to the Thuchi") he would not

POLITICAL FUNCTIONS OF AGE ORGANIZATION 135

hesitate to take it and would administer it to the best of his ability.

Not very long afterwards Chief M'Imathiu was killed in attempting to arrest a dangerous maniac. There was some suggestion of foul play but it was not substantiated. No doubt, however, many Igembe thought that M'Imathiu's death was the work of the original commination sworn by Gwantai some thirty years before, especially as his successor belonged to Michubu (Ntiba).

In the untouched system the differentiation between the ruling sets and the rest was of more relevance to participation in ritual than in tribal decisions. But the ruling set or generation had certain privileges from which the other sets or generations were excluded. In some cases these privileges could be "bought" by members of the generation not ruling at the time. In Kikuyu, for instance, the right to hold a circumcision at one's homestead is a privilege of the ruling generation. To do so enhances one's prestige. There is also profit in it because the fathers of the candidates each pay a fee to the head of the homestead; this is called *ihithia* and each father is said to *hithia mwana* ('pay for the concealing of the child'). A similar expression is used of goats put in the charge of someone else (*hithia mburi kwa ng'ania*, 'cause goats to be hidden with So-and-So', i.e. send goats to be looked after by him). In Karura it is generally held that before a man who is not of the ruling generation can hold a circumcision ceremony at his homestead he must pay what is sometimes reckoned as an *ituika* fee, *mburi ya ndegwa* ('goat of the ox') or *ndegwa ya kuambatira* ('ox for moving up') and the *horio* ('cooling') ram. The former, however, would not appear to be strictly an *ituika* fee since it is held by many that another *mburi ya ndegwa* or *ya ituika* will have to be paid at the

136   KIKUYU SOCIAL AND POLITICAL INSTITUTIONS

actual *ituika*. Rather does it correspond to the *mburi ya ndundu* ('goat of the secret session') of Metume and Gaki, which, together with the *mburi ya mukuha* ('goat of the bodkin', signifying the 'implement of binding') also payable in Karura, entitles a man to join in the legislative functions of the ruling generation, provided that he is a member of the *kiama* proper and in Gaki has paid the fee called *mburi ya kirige* ('goat of the staff of office').[1] The *mukuha* fee is sometimes known as the *mburi ya ndukanio* ('goat for the mixing') which is also used as the name for the fee payable by a man who goes to live on another man's land. Payment is actually made in goats, sheep, oxen or beer, the amounts varying from clan to clan. The *ndundu* fee in one particular instance was four *itumbi* (large gourds) of *njohi* (sugar-cane beer) and a quantity of *njahi* (dolichos beans) and *uchuru* (gruel). These same payments (*ndundu* and *mukuha*) entitle a man in Metume and Gaki to hold circumcision ceremonies at his homestead. No payments, however, can buy the right to a man to take part in the tribal sacrifices appropriate to the ruling generation, except in the special case where someone has deliberately or inadvertently taken some share in such a sacrifice. He is then required to "join" the ruling generation and to swear the oath of secrecy.[2] This change will not affect the generation membership of his sons.

Laws and specific orders are usually proclaimed at

---

[1] Literally 'goat of the roasting fire', from *riga*, used originally for 'burn off the skin' of a wild animal intended for food. It is the fee payable when the *muthigi* and *matathi* are issued to the novice.

[2] A common African method of preserving the secrecy of a society or lodge is to require the trespasser to join and so subject himself to the power of a potent oath. It is said in Meru that the victims of the Athi witchcraft society were promptly initiated for this purpose, but that the punishment for prying on the Njuri Ncheke was death. But one instance is related in which a woman was initiated into this lodge because she was found trying to eavesdrop.

POLITICAL FUNCTIONS OF AGE ORGANIZATION 137

public meetings by *athamaki* or *agambi* of the ruling generation or set supported by those of the other alternation. The opportunity is sometimes taken to make such proclamations at a spectacular dance (like the *kibata* of Kikuyu and Embu or the *authi* of Meru) likely to attract a great number of the general population. They may also be made at meetings of the men, which in Kikuyu are specially convened by the leading *muthamaki's muhuhi wa choro* (trumpet blower); the *choro* is a special ceremonial trumpet made of the horn of an *ndongoro* (greater kudu).[1] Proclamations are often made during the *ituika* (*ntuiko*). Formerly there was an attempt at "cleaning up" the country just before the replacement of one set or generation by the next; outstanding claims (particularly for compensation in respect of homicides) were quickly settled and habitual thieves were hunted down and dealt with. It is said that in Meru warnings were broadcast that unless such claims were brought for settlement before the *ntuiko* ceremonies, they would not be entertained. There was thus in theory a sort of limitation; a suit was barred by time if an *ntuiko* had intervened. But the limitation was largely disregarded and was possibly merely symptomatic of the usual feeling between *nthuki* (sets). However that may be, the country was theoretically "cleaned up", and in all the tribes the new rulers started their period of power with a clean bill of political health and usually set out to emphasize their power by proclamations, frequently no more than reiterations or slight amendments of earlier statutes. The word for a law or order so proclaimed is *muhingo* (pl. *mihingo*) in Kikuyu, *mubingo* in Ndia, Gichugu, Embu, Mbere and Chuka and *mwingo* in the Meru group.

[1] In Meru the trumpet is called *rugoji* and the animal *kamaru*. Originally each *gaaru* had its *rugoji*.

K

138 KIKUYU SOCIAL AND POLITICAL INSTITUTIONS

The sanctions in support of these laws are largely of a supernatural nature. Those proclaimed at a stage in the *ituika* at which the incoming set or generation can be deemed to have assumed administrative power are sufficiently supported by the *ituika* sacrifices. In Embu, for instance, acceptance of a new law is demonstrated on such occasions by a slow and rhythmical clapping of hands by the public present. At other times special sacrifices may be made. Thus in Mwimbi an oath similar to the *nkumbuko* oath[1] may be sworn by *nkome* elders on behalf of the people of the area concerned, and is considered to involve the death of any one of them who disobeys the law proclaimed. Sometimes in Chuka a ceremonial fire is started by *nkome* elders and everybody present throws a stick or twig on it, the elders declaring that the law-breaker will be similarly consumed. Such special oaths, however, like the secret oath of *kathaka kai* ('the evil little bushland') in Meru proper, particularly Tigania and Igembe, are used only in very special circumstances. In the main the laws are supported by the sanctions inherent in the right to rule acknowledged at the *ituika* and exercised in the associated tribal sacrifices.

The punishment for disobeying a law is usually a "fine" of one ram in Kikuyu and one ram or bull in Meru. The "fine" is eaten by the elders. Persistent disobedience or failure to pay the "fine" was formerly dealt with by the warriors and junior grades, accompanied by elders, a larger "fine" being collected forcibly or the crops of the delinquent being cut down.

The area of operation of a law is the area of jurisdiction of the elders taking part in the proclamation. Co-ordination is effected by previous meetings at which agreement has been reached, proclamations being issued subsequently

[1] See above, p. 125.

POLITICAL FUNCTIONS OF AGE ORGANIZATION 139

and more or less simultaneously in the various areas. This method can be illustrated for all the tribes by a description of it as applied to Meru. The body empowered to legislate for a village group (*mwiriga*) is its *njuri*, in theory the elders of the ruling set who are *njuri* members, but in practice only in liaison with *njuri* members of the other age-division. Legislation for two or more *miiriga* is a function of the *njuri* of them all, but in practice not all the members will take part. A number of *agambi* of both age-divisions will represent the various *miiriga*. If the area is still wider (say the whole of Miiriga Mieru or Abothu-guchi) representation will be by *agambi* chosen by the *agambi*; the representatives are then *agambi* (spokesmen) of the *agambi* of the *miiriga*. And so on. Finally the whole tribe might be represented by an *nkireba* (select committee, secret session) of *agambi* of *agambi* of *agambi* . . . of *agambi* of the numerous *miiriga*, which group themselves in larger and larger units for the purposes of tribal legislation. The final *nkireba* must represent both age-divisions. No *njuri* member is excluded, but unwieldiness is avoided by a series of agreements and selections in the manner indicated.[1] In practice it is the most renowned among the numerous *agambi* who constitute the final *nkireba* which a Meru might then describe as *nkireba ya Kiruka na Ntiba ya ome ba biongo bia agambi ba njuri ya kiama* ('select committee of Kiruka and Ntiba of the wise men from among the leaders of the spokesmen of the senior lodge'). All areas are represented because the manner of selection involves the grouping of small areas into larger ones, these into larger ones again, and so on. A Meru local government

---

[1] It appears that eight was formerly considered the proper (though not obligatory) number of *agambi* for any two disputing units (i.e. four from each) smaller than a sub-tribe. Sub-tribes were usually represented by eight from each.

140 KIKUYU SOCIAL AND POLITICAL INSTITUTIONS

would be constituted on these lines, and no form of local government devised for Meru would satisfy the Meru legislative theory unless it were so constituted. But membership of a Meru *nkireba* is by no means fixed and constant; representation is by institutions, not by individuals; the number of the individuals actually attending as spokesmen of the institution may be whittled down to two (one of each age-division) although the area covered by the institution may be very wide. But they are not thereby appointed as the permanent representatives of their area. At the next meeting of the *nkireba* the spokesmen of the institution may be two other *agambi* altogether or one or both may be the same. There is no system of election or selection for a term of office or even for a class of work. But in practice the same men, who are the recognized *ome ba biongo bia agambi*, will regularly attend.

There is some variation between tribes as to matters concerning which the legislative authorities are deemed to have power. The Kikuyu of Karura hold that purely domestic affairs, among which they include the rate of "bride-price", are outside their scope. "Bride-price", they say, is a matter of arrangement between the families of the bride and bridegroom, and the elders cannot interfere by making rules. The Kikuyu of Metume, however, put the matter on a different basis altogether. They say that no proclamation can regulate the relative values as assessed in goats (for purposes of exchange) of heifers, girls, and land. These, the exchange of which was formerly governed by the customary rules pertaining to *uthoni* (controlled intimacy between families or clans) are the *indo chia nduire* ('things of long standing'), by which they do not mean that their exchange values are fixed by long usage (which in fact they are not) but that the things themselves are those on which the family or clan depends

POLITICAL FUNCTIONS OF AGE ORGANIZATION 141

for its immortality on earth. "Land," the Metume elders say, "owned by the clan, means a place to live for ever, girls are the means by which the clan perpetuates itself, and cows by providing calves provide the means to get the goats to get the girls. The perpetuance of the clan depends on these three things. They are the *indo chia mindi na mindi* ('things for the ever and ever') and no tribal law can come between two clans concerned with mutual arrangements for their own persistence."

The Tharaka, Chuka, Muthambi, Mwimbi, Igoji and Miutini also hold that no legislative body can interfere with "bride-price" and the Meru tend to do the same, though some believe that the insistence of the elders on a uniform payment is evidence that this was fixed by proclamation many years ago; others however assert that this is merely a rejection of the new principle of actual purchase of girls which is liable to creep in from other tribes in which the payments back and forth from clan to clan are not so nicely balanced.

But the Embu are an exception. There the elders definitely hold that the rate of "bride-price" can be changed by proclamation. They say that the oldest rate remembered was three heifers and two bulls and that this was subsequently changed to two heifers and two bulls and afterwards changed back again. But they agree that the second change was not operative all through the tribe; the Andu a Muthanga in particular still pay four beasts only and receive the same amount. It is possible, however, that this is a pseudo-historical interpretation of changes which came about for other reasons. However that may be the Embu are quite certain that the ruling generation, in consultation with the other members of the senior *kiama* grade, have the power to vary "bride-price" and in fact have done so. The elders of Gichugu and Ndia affirm

142 KIKUYU SOCIAL AND POLITICAL INSTITUTIONS

with equal certainty that in their sections of Kikuyu there is no such power.

The Metume elders gave the following instances of the purposes for which orders could be and to their personal knowledge had from time to time been proclaimed:

The Prevention of Witchcraft

A general proclamation against the use of witchcraft and outlawry of all witchdoctors. The type of punishment to be inflicted, e.g. death by choking. Occasional orders to the *aanake* to round-up all alleged witch-doctors.

The Prevention of Theft

Outlawry of habitual thieves and occasional orders for their rounding-up. The manner of their execution. The use of *aanake* to put a stop to highway robbery.

The Prevention of Famine

Orders for the conservation of certain kinds of foodstuffs during a threat of famine. Orders against the harvesting of immature crops. Orders permitting the peaceful entry of people of a starving tribe (e.g. Kamba) in search of food. The proclamation of a truce with an enemy tribe during a period of famine.

The Reservation of Land for Public Purposes

Orders declaring an open space to be a *kiharo* (public meeting place), orders requiring a salt-lick to be open to the public, orders to prevent destruction of forest areas required as protective belts against outside aggression, the dedication of paths, fords, and watering-places for public use, and the like. Orders regulating the collection of firewood from protective belts, the collection being done by

POLITICAL FUNCTIONS OF AGE ORGANIZATION 143

an *itua* (company) of *airitu* and *aanake*, the latter as an escort to the former.

The following examples illustrate the kind of orders issued in recent years:

Gichugu and Ndia

(1) If a man lives with a girl apparently intending to marry her, but fails to do so he will have to pay "for the virginity". (This order was passed on by Mwangi to Irungu at the *ituika* and was reiterated by the Irungu in 1938.)

Embu

(1) An order to prevent the introduction of the Kikuyu practice of *ngwiko*. (Date not known. Said to be about 1910.)

(2) *Right to Children.* Formerly the children of a marriage invariably belonged to their mother if the marriage was dissolved, the father receiving back his original "bride-price" together with its offspring, provided that he could swear an oath as to its whereabouts. Henceforth, if the woman is to blame for the divorce, the husband retains the children and the wife's father the "bride price" and its offspring. (Passed in 1932.)

(3) An order requiring the noxious weed called Mexican marigold to be uprooted wherever found in Embu territory. (Passed in 1932.)

(4) An order limiting the operation of "female circumcision" to an incision of sufficient depth and extent for the removal of the glans clitoridis only. (Passed in 1932.)

Chuka

(1) As in Embu (4)

(2) An order requiring girls to be initiated in early adolescence (if at all). (Passed in 1934.)

Mwimbi

(1) As in Embu (4).

(2) As in Chuka (2). (This had already been passed in a similar form in Upper Mwimbi about 1908.)

(3) An order forbidding the practice of the cult of *ukiama*. (Passed in 1940.)

Tharaka

(1) An order forbidding the enclosure of grazing areas for individual use as *icheche*, like the Kamba *isese*. (Date not known.)

Meru Proper

(1) An order requiring the proper burial of deceased persons. (Passed in 1934.)

(2) As in Chuka (2).

(3) An order prohibiting the practice of the Athi witchcraft cult (Igembe only). (Passed in 1940.)

(4) An order fixing the relative values of stock assessed in goats, including the value of a prospective heifer calf exchanged in the original customary manner. (Passed in 1942.)

(5) An order instituting compensation of one ox payable to her father by a man who causes the pregnancy of an initiated unmarried girl (*ngutu*). This order was rendered necessary by the earlier initiation of girls. (Passed in 1942.)

(6) An order that the penalty for misappropriation of cash by a man to whom it has been entrusted shall not be less than that customarily imposed for misappropriation of other forms of property. (Passed in 1942.)

The orders shown as Embu (4) and Chuka (2) were inspired by District Commissioners, but were issued by the indigenous legislative bodies after the latter had expressed agreement with the principles involved.

INDEX

Adult *kiama*. *See Kiama*.
Adultery, 34
Age, terms denoting, 2, 3ff.
Age-divisions, 10, 11, 42, 43-4, 63, 131, 132, 133. *See also* Generations.
  mates, 2, 54, 66
  sets, 1, 2, 6, 8, 11, 12ff., 26, 27, 32ff., 47, 48, 66, 67, 81, 97, 104, 133, 135, 139. *See also* Circumcision, Initiation.
    girls', 20, 32, 34, 36-7, 38
    names of, 9ff, 14, 15, 21, 22, 24, 25, 26, 33, 35-9, 44, 48, 49, 51-2, 97
    pre-initiation, 32ff., 73ff.
    women's, 2, 19, 38-9, 51, 52
  status, 3, 6, 90
Amathaki. *See Muthamaki*.

Bride, 6, 7, 55, 82, 140
Bride-price, 114, 140, 141, 143

Chiefs, 63, 105, 132, 133, 134, 135
Child, children, 3-5, 6, 7, 23, 32-4, 80, 83, 87, 88, 90, 92, 99, 102, 143
Childbirth, 99
Chuka, 1, 3, 4, 6, 42, 44, 46-7, 74, 76, 78, 79, 82-3, 92, 94, 137, 138, 141, 143-4
Cicatrization, 5, 96
Circumcision, 4, 12, 13, 22, 27, 32, 34, 43, 53, 66, 69, 80, 88, 90, 103, 104, 135, 136. *See also* Initiation.
  in Embu, 23, 24, 25
  in Meru, 27, 29, 81, 95
  of girls, 4, 95, 99, 143. *See also* Clitoridectomy.
  prohibition of, 10, 12, 14, 15, 57
Clan, 4, 47, 102, 107-8, 113, 114, 116, 118, 124, 125, 126, 127, 131, 136, 140-1

Clitoridectomy, 5, 36, 96, 143
Compensation, 92, 113-14, 115ff., 124, 125, 131, 137, 144
Corpses, 92-3, 100
Courts, 57, 109ff., 117, 118, 121, 122, 127, 129, 130

Dances, 56, 57, 58, 69, 76, 86, 87, 102-3, 137

Elders, 6, 10, 11, 19, 23, 40, 44, 48, 50, 57, 58, 60, 61-2, 63ff., 67, 69, 75, 88, 89, 104, 117, 121, 124, 126, 130f., 138, 141. *See also* Generations.
  institutions of, 80ff. *See also* Lodges.
Embu, 1, 8, 24, 42ff., 83, 94, 129, 138, 141, 143
  'handing over' ceremony in, 62-3
  regimental system in, 23ff.
Europeans, 9, 12, 19, 58, 105, 114, 118, 121

Family, 2, 61, 107, 114, 129, 140
Famine, 9, 13, 18, 19, 43, 44, 142
Fees, for entry into grades or lodges, 34, 56-7, 74-6, 78, 80, 84ff., 135-6
  in judicial actions, 108, 110, 111
  payable at 'handing over' ceremony, 60-1, 62
  payable by regiments, 70
Fines, 98, 113, 138

Gaaru (barracks), 76, 77, 80
Generation(s), 40ff., 61, 62, 63
  cycle, 41-2, 45, 48-50
  divisions, 42-3, 44, 45, 47, 48
  names, 41, 43, 45ff.
  ruling, 58-60, 61, 69, 131, 135ff., 141
Githaka (land of homestead), 2

148 KIKUYU SOCIAL AND POLITICAL INSTITUTIONS

Githitu (sacred military objects), 71, 72
Guthiga ceremony, 34, 53

Homestead, 2, 95, 102, 125, 129, 135, 136
Homicide, 83, 92, 109, 115, 116, 118, 123, 124, 137

Imenti, 27, 28, 29, 31, 35, 37, 49, 65, 75, 90, 96, 126
Initiation, 1, 2, 5, 8, 12, 15, 17, 23, 24, 33, 34, 36, 54-5, 57, 66, 73, 89, 92. *See also* Circumcision.
  of girls, 4, 5, 6, 25, 34, 36, 55, 96, 144
  pre-initiation lodges, 73ff.
Insignia (of leaders), 106
Ituika ('handing over' ceremony), 42, 58-60, 135, 137
  in Chuka, 42
  in Embu, 42, 60-4
  in Meru, 48, 132-3
  in Mwimbi, 65

Judicial system, 83-4, 104, 107ff., 110-12, 117, 118-22, 130. *See also* Courts.

Kamba, 2, 53, 105
Kiama (*Chiama*). *See* Lodges.
Kikuyu Land Unit, 1, 3, 40, 74, 76, 94, 123
  sub-tribes, 1, 29, 30, 35, 36, 49, 82-3, 92, 94, 95, 97
Kinship, kinsmen, 47, 107, 108, 110, 114, 115, 118, 120, 121, 127, 128

Leaders, leadership, 58, 74, 84, 97, 100ff., 109, 110, 111, 116, 117, 120, 121, 131, 133, 137, 139
Legislation, 100, 105, 120, 131ff., 137, 139, 140-1, 142-4
Lodges, 73ff., 108, 115, 116, 123, 128, 129, 131, 136, 139, 141
  for adults, 81, 82, 83

for boys, 74, 75, 76, 103, 104
for elders, 80ff., 84, 92, 131
grades of, 82-4, 90ff., 94, 131
in Meru, 90ff., 131, 139
payments to, 84ff. *See also* Fees.
warriors', 76
women's, 95-8

Magic of numbers, 8, 13, 17, 119
Marriage, 4, 15, 36, 37, 51, 54, 61, 66, 67, 80-1, 87, 102, 143
Masai, 9, 11, 70
Masturbation, 54, 56 and note
Mathira, 14-15, 71
Mbere, 24, 25, 44, 46, 62, 83, 91, 94
Menstruation, 6, 23, 34, 55, 86
Meru, 1, 2, 3, 5-7, 47, 48, 49, 74, 81, 95, 100, 106, 113, 127, 129, 132, 139, 144
  age-sets in, 35ff.
  njuri, 90ff., 94, 139
  regimental system, 26ff., 35, 47, 97
  women's lodges, 96-8
Mugambi. *See* Leaders.
Muthamaki. *See* Leaders.

Ntuika. *See Ituika*.

Oaths, 57, 58, 64, 71, 91, 98, 99, 122-7, 132, 134, 136, 138
Ordeals, 122-3

Patrilineal descent, 1, 44, 80, 117, 125
Political organization, 1, 40, 59-60, 65, 69, 73ff., 105, 132-5, 137
  Chuka, 46
  Embu, 62
  Meru, 47, 49, 140
Pregnancy, 55, 79, 144
Pre-initiation age-sets, 32ff.
  institutions, 73ff.
Procreation, 66
Property, 114, 115, 118, 122, 130, 140-1, 144
Puberty, 23, 24

Rape, 53-4, 55-6

INDEX 149

Regiments, 1, 2, 8ff., 19, 69-72
  dates of, 11, 19-22
  formation of, 14, 16, 17, 18, 27
  in Embu, 23ff.
  in Meru, 26ff.
  in Tetu, 10-12, 21
  names of, 9, 10, 14, 15, 16, 20, 21, 27, 28-9
Rituals, 53ff., 135

Sacrifices, 44, 57, 58, 59, 61, 63, 64, 89, 92, 95, 100, 123, 126, 136, 138

Territorial organization, 2, 61, 94-5, 105, 108, 138-9, 140

Tetu, 10, 71
  regimental system in, 11, 13, 14, 21, 22
Tharaka, 6, 31, 43, 65, 81, 92, 141, 144
Theft, 119, 142

Village, 2
  group, 2, 139
Virginity, 55, 143

Warfare, 70ff., 77, 78, 105, 116, 118
Warriors, 5, 8, 23, 32, 37, 47, 48, 56, 57, 65, 69, 77, 80, 85, 87, 96, 104, 116, 129, 138
  institutions of, 76, 78, 79
Witchcraft, 79, 125, 134, 142, 144
Women's lodges, 95-100